BUNK 9's GUIDE to GROWING UP

Secrets, Tips, and Expert Advice on the GOOD 😃, the BAD 😣 & the AWKWARD 😐

All about your changing body from the girls of ★ CAMP SILVER MOON ★

As told to Adah Nuchi
Illustrated by Meg Hunt

Dr. Meryl Newman-Cedar, Medical Consultant

WORKMAN PUBLISHING ⚡ NEW YORK

For the members of my own Sisterhood, who make being a woman that much more fun. —A. N.

Library of Congress Cataloging-in-Publication Data is available.

PAPERBACK ISBN 978-0-7611-9359-2   HARDCOVER ISBN 978-1-5235-0268-4

Workman books are available at special discounts when purchased in bulk for premiums and sales promotions as well as for fund-raising or educational use. Special editions or book excerpts can also be created to specification. For details, contact the Special Sales Director at the address below, or send an email to specialmarkets@workman.com.

WORKMAN PUBLISHING CO., INC.

225 Varick Street, New York, NY 10014

workman.com

Printed in China   First printing November 2017   10 9 8 7 6 5 4 3 2 1

Editor: Justin Krasner   Designer: Carolyn Bahar

Art Director: Colleen AF Venable   Production Editor: Beth Levy

Production Manager: Julie Primavera

This book is meant to be used as *an additional resource* and should not replace the guidance of or treatment by a doctor or other health care professional.

DEAR PARENTS AND OTHER TRUSTED ADULTS:

We know, WE KNOW... we're supposed to write you a real letter about how we passed the advanced swim test (four laps and 120 seconds of treading water!), or how we got "Bunk of the Week" for the cleanest bunk (never in a million years), or to complain about the dining hall's tuna casserole (it's REALLY gross). And we promise, that letter is coming... soon.

But until then, we wanted to let you know that we wrote a book about growing up—you know, PERIODS AND BOOBS AND FEELINGS AND STUFF. It's for the younger girls at Camp Silver Moon (and anyone they give it to), so that they have the information they need about **PUBERTY**. We think YOU should read it too. After all, some of the girls who read it might have questions, and The Book says to come to trusted adults (THAT'S YOU!) with those questions. Plus, if you read it, you'll probably have an easier time starting the *conversation* yourself. And, let's be honest, you might even learn a thing or two...

So if you see a girl from Camp Silver Moon (or a girl who knows a girl who knows a girl from Camp Silver Moon) reading this book, feel free to borrow it. Just make sure you give it back!

Sincerely,

Bunk 9

P.S. Please bring Chinese food on Visiting Day.
P.P.S. Also bring magazines!

CONT

ENTS

welcome to
BUNK 9!

CONGRATULATIONS! You have found... The Book.
No, not just ANY book: Bunk 9's Guide to Growing Up:
Secrets, Tips, and Expert Advice on the Good, the Bad & the
Awkward. We admit the title is a bit of a mouthful. Which is
why, from this moment on, it will hereby be known as The Book.

If you're wondering why you're holding The Book, here are
a few possible reasons:

1. You are a camper at Camp Silver Moon and you live in
   Bunk 9.
2. You are a camper at Camp Silver Moon and you don't live
   in Bunk 9, but one of your friends does and she gave you
   The Book.
3. You have no idea what Bunk 9 or Camp Silver Moon is, but
   someone gave you The Book and you would like to know the
   secrets, tips, and expert advice on the GOOD, the
   BAD, and the AWKWARD.
4. You stole The Book from your sister.
5. Other: _____

(FILL IN THE BLANK)

6

If you're wondering how The Book came to be, well, you could say that **it's all LEA'S FAULT**. See, there were always *eight* of us: Abby, Brianna, Emma L., Emma R., Grace, Jenna, Makayla, and Sage. All the bunks at Camp Silver Moon hold eight campers. Four bunk beds in a neat square, and a counselor area in the back. EXCEPT the CIT bunks (for you newbies, that's Counselor In Training, aka the sixteen-year-olds, aka the oldest kids at camp, aka what we are now), which have *eight single beds*.

CIT bed

Bunk 9 bed

VS.

They're **REAL** beds too. No saggy springs and plastic-covered mattresses. Or so we hear...

Because this year, **LEA SHOWED UP**.

Normally, this wouldn't be a problem. You squeeze in one extra bed, and voilà! But not in the CIT bunk. There an extra bed is a fire hazard. So what did the camp director do? Instead of saying, "Sorry, Lea, no room for you," she stuck us all in Bunk 9, which

I formally object to being treated like the villain of this story.
—Lea

is normally reserved for the twelve-year-old girls, and sent the Twelves to live the life of luxury. Did the CIT boys suffer the same fate? NOPE! They're happily waking up without banging their heads on the bed above.

WHAM!

OUCH!

Let's just say we were all prepared to **HATE** Lea.

7

OF COURSE, from the moment we met her it was clear she was a member of the **SILVER MOON SISTERHOOD**.

She just has that *je ne sais quoi* that makes her impossible to hate. It helps that she's French—and that she brought us chocolate from France.

Thank you!
—Lea

HEY!! It's my insomnia!
—Brianna

Besides, once we were actually in Bunk 9, it really wasn't SO BAD. True, it's not great when Brianna is tossing and turning in the bed above you. And now that we're not right next door to the BOYS, it's almost impossible to sneak into their bunk at night and reset their alarm clocks for 5 a.m. But we'll take Lea over single beds and pranking the boys any day of the week.

Plus, **being in Bunk 9 reminded us of the summer we were all TWELVE.** The summer when we threw Emma L. a period party, Grace tried—unsuccessfully—to **STUFF HER BRA**, and Abby had her *first kiss*. We thought of all the things we know now that we wish we had known then (there were a lot of them), and that's when we got the idea for The Book. We wanted the girls of Bunk 9 (you know, once it returns to its rightful occupants—YOU!) to be armed with the information they needed to be ready for *womanhood*. So we decided to write everything down and hide The Book in Bunk 9. Which, if you're reading this—drumroll, please—you have now found!

So if you're wondering about the hair that's growing down there, or when your boobs will start growing up here, or if you don't know what to do about your... PERIOD (just kidding! It's "period"—lowercase—even if it sometimes feels like it should be in all caps), WE'RE HERE TO HELP. Because if we had a lot of questions (How exactly do you put on a bra?), you probably do too. And things might be kind of confusing. (Why are there SO many different kinds of pads?) And all those unknowns can even be a little bit scary. (That tampon is supposed to go WHERE?)

But take it from us: While there are a whole lot of changes that happen on the road to womanhood, they're all leading somewhere completely wonderful. (And once you get the hang of them, tampons aren't scary at all.) So that's where The Book comes in. We're here to walk you through the process, head to toe, of all of these changes called *puberty*. And while we're at it, we'll throw in some tips and advice on how to take care of yourself now that you're growing older, so that you'll not only survive puberty; you'll completely, totally, 100 percent own it.

9

So without further ado, we hereby initiate you into the **SILVER MOON SISTERHOOD.** The following pages contain *magical* (and non-magical) secrets, tips, and expert advice for girls on the good, the bad, and the awkward, as compiled by the CITs of Bunk 9. GUARD THIS BOOK WITH YOUR LIFE, and use its secrets wisely.

xoxo,

The ~~girls~~ **WOMEN** of Bunk 9

Makayla   Abby   Lea   EMMA L.   Brianna
       Emma R.   SAGE   GRACE   Jenna

P.S. Once you commit this book to memory, please leave it for the next girls. They need to know the secrets too! Unless of course you don't live in Bunk 9, in which case this book is yours to keep.

P.P.S. If you have any secrets, tips, and advice that we didn't think of, add them in the margins. Knowledge is power!*

*If The Book made its way to a library (SO EMBARRASSING!) please do not write, scribble, or draw in it.

...and here are the

LADIES OF BUNK 9

at age twelve!

Brianna

social butterfly ✶ night
owl ✶ racoonophobe
HOMETOWN: AUSTIN, TX

Abby

aspiring chef ✶ dancing
queen ✶ late bloomer
HOMETOWN: EUGENE, OR

EMMA L.

science whiz ✶ Ropes Course
pro ✶ avocado aficionado
HOMETOWN: NEW YORK, NY

Emma R.

early bird ✶ bunk
"mom" ✶ zen yogi
HOMETOWN: SAN JOSE, CA

GRACE

volleyball prodigy ✶ bookworm
✶ BeDazzler extraordinaire
HOMETOWN: PRINCETON, NJ

SAGE

track star ✶ Earth saver
✶ veggie fanatic
HOMETOWN: EUGENE, OR

Jenna

music fan ✶ aspiring actress
✶ proud exercise avoider
HOMETOWN: PHILADELPHIA, PA

Makayla

lake lover ✶ expert bra
shopper ✶ boys' bunk spy
HOMETOWN: CHARLOTTE, NC

Lea

chocolate connoisseur ✶ foreign
correspondent ✶ Ropes Course objector
HOMETOWN: PARIS, FRANCE

Camp Silver Moon
WEEK 1

IN WHICH BRIANNA AND ABBY NOTICE THAT **SOMETHING IS DIFFERENT,** AND EVERYONE WONDERS IF THINGS WILL EVER BE THE SAME.

The summer we were twelve may have been our fourth one at Camp Silver Moon, but it was clear from the moment the camp bus pulled into the parking lot that THIS SUMMER WOULD BE DIFFERENT. Brianna, Emma R., and Jenna were there waiting to meet us—their parents had dropped them off an hour or so earlier—and when the rest of us tumbled off the bus, they stood by the side of the road with signs that read "BUNK 9," like chauffeurs at an airport. OK, maybe they were hopping up and down, not standing. (They would have made *terrible* chauffeurs.) But we were ALL jumping. We were home.

Abby was the first one to reach them. She ran straight to Brianna, who picked her up in a big, giant hug. **And BOOM! Everything was different.** Sure, Brianna had always been taller than Abby, but now she towered above her. And it wasn't just the height difference. Next to Brianna, Abby looked like a STICK FIGURE. She was all limbs poking out of the holes of her clothes. Brianna, on the other hand, had hips. And BOOBS.

The differences were *everywhere*, especially on the tops of our cubbies. Makayla set up a collection of pads on hers. A collection that most definitely wasn't there the summer

before. Grace set up a collection of Nancy Drew books. (Somewhere in Paris, Lea was reading the same mysteries. Only her heroine was named Alice Roy.) Emma R. displayed a stick of deodorant. Sage displayed a pack of cards. Emma L. had a little razor. Jenna had a little photograph of her dog.

When we changed into our bathing suits for Swim, it was impossible not to notice that suddenly the girls of Bunk 9 had *pubic hair*—well, half of them did. It was also impossible not to notice that half of us smelled different. And had ZITS. Some of us were envious and some of us didn't care. Some of us wished our armpits would sprout hair, and some of us wished our periods had never come. But there was one thing we were all worried about: With so many changes,

COULD THE GIRLS OF BUNK 9 STAY FRIENDS?
OR
WOULD THIS BE THE SUMMER THAT TORE US APART?

14

Confession Time

A couple of us (AHEM, Abby and Sage) showed up to Camp Silver Moon that summer and had no idea what puberty was.

Sure, they knew that their moms had different bodies than they did, and they could connect the dots enough to understand that their bodies would be different one day too (after all, our bodies have been changing since before we were born!), but they never bothered to wonder about **how one got from point A to point B.** And the fact that this journey had a name? Whoa!

A ✧ PUBERTY ✧ B

Not that anyone holds it against them. They were busy doing other things. But just in case you're also reading this, scratching your head, and thinking, "Puber-HUH?," we want to start at the very beginning.

> Yup! That summer I was so, so, so far from puberty that it wasn't anywhere near my radar. Luckily I had my bunkmates to fill me in, so when it was FINALLY my turn, I knew exactly what was coming. —Abby

> OK, true: I didn't know what puberty was. But that's because I was too busy kicking major butt on the track team to wonder about those bumps that had popped up on my chest. —SAGE

PUBERTY: THE VERY BEGINNING

You've probably noticed that your body is constantly changing. Every year you grow taller, you gain weight, your feet get bigger, your arms and legs get longer. Even your facial features change! Usually those changes happen slowly (though sometimes, like when you're having a growth spurt, they seem as if they happen overnight). But at some point, your body begins to change in new and (mostly) exciting ways. Some of these changes (like breast growth) happen on the outside, some of them (like an increase in hormones) happen on the inside, and some (like new feelings and emotions) aren't physical at all. But put them all together, and they spell **PUBERTY** (that's PYOO-ber-tee). In other words, puberty is all of the changes your body goes through on **THE ROAD TO BECOMING AN ADULT.**

EMMA L.'S SCIENCE CORNER

Hormones are chemicals found in the body naturally. Among other things, they affect how you change and grow. When you go through puberty, the hormones in your body increase. If you've noticed that you sweat more, or that you might not smell so fresh, you can blame hormones. And those zits sprouting on your face? You guessed it: **HORMONES.**

That road to becoming an adult? That's what being a teenager is!
—Makayla

16

CH-CH-CH- CHANGES!

(OR, WHAT'S GOING TO HAPPEN, FROM THE OUTSIDE IN)

For most girls, puberty starts sometime between the ages of eight and fourteen (give or take). The key word in that sentence? <u>START</u>. We are very happy to report that all of these changes don't happen at once, and they *definitely* don't happen overnight. The whole process of puberty, from start to finish, can take two years, five years, or anywhere in between, and changes occur in spurts and at different times.

> I knew what puberty was, but I didn't know how it happened. Or how long it would take! I really thought that I would wake up one morning with a brand-new body. Am I disappointed? A little bit. Am I relieved? You bet.
> —Jenna

> Age is but a number! If you start noticing breast growth before age eight, or (like me) reach age fourteen with nary a boob in sight, then you may fall on the early or late side. But except in extreme cases, you probably have nothing to worry about.
> —Abby

The changes that happen on the outside will be the most obvious, because you'll be able to see them. (OK, you won't be able to see them WHILE they happen, but if you snap a picture of yourself every six months during puberty, we promise they will be noticeable.) To know what you can expect as you take the journey from point A to point B, we turn to Lea for an illustrated demonstration:

next page! **17**

Before you start puberty, you'll look like you're used to looking!

But at some point you might see tiny hairs on your legs and under your arms. Your armpits might also start smelling. And you'll notice two bumps on your chest. Those are your breasts starting to grow.

You'll also sprout a few pubic hairs. These might not match the color or texture of the hair on you head and often start off thin and straight before getting thicker and more curly.

If it seems as if EVERYTHING is growing, that's because it is! Your hips will get wider, your breasts will continue to grow, you'll get taller, and you'll gain weight. Oh, and those pubic hairs? They're multiplying!

You'll start growing more underarm hair, you may notice a milky fluid in your underwear (this is called vaginal discharge), and soon you'll start menstruating (that's your period).

Growth slows down once you get your period, but it may take a few years before you stop growing. How many years? I'm STILL growing, and I have no idea what my future holds!

19

Most girls will notice that their breasts begin to grow first, but no two puberty experiences are the same. You may discover a few pubic hairs before you get boobs. (That's PYOO-bic hair, and it refers to the hair that grows in the triangle between your hips and above and around your vagina. In other words, the area that's covered by the front and bottom of your underwear.) Or you might be tipped off by a sudden growth spurt, a couple of ZITS, or a funky armpit smell. One thing you can count on, though, is that **your period won't be the first change** to hit. So if you haven't noticed any of the signs of puberty yet, you don't have to worry about being caught off guard when you're paddling a canoe in the middle of Lake Silver Moon.

> Guys? Guys? I think I've sprung a leak!

Your outside isn't the only thing that's changing. On the inside, your hormones are working hard. So is your reproductive system (that is, the parts of your body that can one day make a baby, or reproduce): your ovaries, fallopian tubes, uterus, cervix, and vagina. You can't see them, but they look like this:

FALLOPIAN TUBE

FALLOPIAN TUBE

OVARY

OVARY

UTERUS

CERVIX

VAGINA

Until puberty, these parts are just hanging out. But when puberty kicks in, your hormones get to work and your reproductive system goes into operation, preparing your body to be capable of having a baby. MENSTRUATION is the result of all of that preparation. (We'll cover everything you need to know about menstruation—aka your period—later, but for now we'll give you a quick spoiler: IT'S AWESOME.)

As for those nonphysical changes? Hormones also affect your feelings and emotions. You may notice that you're angry or annoyed more often than before, or that things that normally wouldn't bother you now do. The reason? HORMONES! You might also find that you're starting to pay more attention to what the boys are doing in the bunk next door. The reason? HORMONES! 😊

> Don't panic! Just because your body is physically able to have a baby, it doesn't mean you should—or that anyone expects you to! Let's be real: Most of us aren't even ready to BABYSIT. This is just one of those cases where your body is getting a loooooooong head start.
> —Makayla

> It's true: As you go through puberty, you'll probably find that you're starting to look at boys—or possibly girls—in a whole new way. But not having those feelings is perfectly fine too. No two people are alike, so try not to worry about how you measure up. —Emma R.

> Good news: If it sounds like puberty is more trouble than it's worth, just know that once you finish going through it, everything calms down. At least a little bit!
> —SAGE

So Will We All End Up Looking Like Lea?

As gorgeous as Lea is, life would be **BORING** if we all looked exactly the same. Luckily, just like everyone starts out looking different, they end up looking different as well. Don't believe us? **Look at BUNK 9!**

at twelve!

at sixteen!

CHANGE, CHANGE, GO AWAY DON'T COME BACK ANOTHER DAY

With so many changes, when it comes to puberty you might be thinking to yourself, "Thanks, but NO thanks." And even though we think becoming a woman is pretty great, we get it: **CHANGE IS HARD.** As hard as getting across Camp Silver Moon's Ropes Course. But just like there's no avoiding the Ropes Course Challenge (as much as some of us try), there's no avoiding puberty, either. Of course, if you're secretly referring to puberty as "The Thing That Shall Not Be Named," we have a few tips to make it better on the next page.

Ropes Course Challenge?! I'm afraid of heights; I don't feel well; I only have one shoe; there's an emergency in the dining hall and I'm needed IMMEDIATELY.
—Lea

I just want you all to know that I would never, ever avoid the Ropes Course Challenge.
—EMMA L.

Puberty can be hard for anyone, but all of the physical changes can be especially hard if it feels like the sex you were born as (that is female or male), doesn't match the gender you identify with. If you feel more comfortable expressing your gender differently, talk to a trusted adult who can help you find the support you need.

TOP THREE TIPS
for the BEST PUBERTY EVER!
(WHEN YOU DON'T WANT PUBERTY AT ALL)

1. Find someone older (and wiser) to talk to. If you're dreading puberty, it may be because you have a lot of unanswered questions. Luckily, billions of women have paved the road ahead of you. TALK TO SOMEONE YOU TRUST— your mom, your best friend's mom, your older sister, your babysitter, your cousin, your aunt Edna, or all of the above. They can probably tell you everything you need to know. And remember, there's NO such thing as a stupid question! —Brianna

I was too embarrassed to talk to my mom about my period, but luckily Emma L.'s mom has always been super easy to talk to. She answered all of my questions, and even called my mom to ask her to buy me pads. —GRACE

And don't rule out dads. Chances are good that your dad or another trusted male adult has done his research and knows what's up. —Emma R.

2. Just because your body is changing, it doesn't mean YOU have to! Your interests might change as you get older, but if you love catching fireflies, hanging from the jungle gym, or reading comic books, you don't have to stop because you've grown a pair of breasts. Make a point of doing the things you love, no matter what's happening on the outside. —SAGE

3. **Find the good in puberty, and focus on that.** You might not love everything about puberty, but you can always find something fun about it. Homemade acne remedies, pretty bras, and keeping a puberty journal are just a few of our favorites. —Makayla

Emma R.'s Tip for Extra-Early Birds

Have you ever heard someone say, "First is the worst, second is the best, third is the one with the hairy chest"? Well, I was first (by A LOT). First to get boobs, first to get underarm hair, first to get my period. Let's just say I wasn't too happy about it. **Not only did I have a ton of questions, but all of my friends kept pointing out my breasts** and asking ME questions! Between my mom and my teacher that year, I got the answers I needed. As for my friends, at first I didn't want to answer their questions ("Get your own boobs!" I wanted to say). But **a lot of the questions they had were the same ones** I had. And it helped to remember that they weren't actually curious about my body; they were curious about their own. After a while, I realized that answering their questions instead of shutting them down meant we had even more to talk about when they started going through puberty themselves. And that made it easier to say, "Yes, it's perfectly normal for your nipples to start sticking out."

OK, but do you *have* to answer other people's questions about your body? **N-0, NO!** It's your body, so you get to decide if you talk about it or not. Whether it's Jenna or your aunt Edna, you only need to talk about it if it feels comfortable to you. Otherwise, practice saying, "I appreciate your curiosity, Aunt Edna, but my period feels personal so I'd prefer if we discuss something else." Of course, your doctor is the exception to that rule. —SAGE

PHEWBERTY!

Then again, if it seems like everyone in the world has breasts except you, when puberty finally does come, it might seem a lot more like PHEWberty. And you don't have to be a late bloomer to be excited for puberty to arrive. (After all, have we mentioned how *awesome* being a woman is? We think we have.) The good news is that just like that Ropes Course Challenge, PUBERTY HAPPENS TO EVERYONE. Eventually. But if you've ever considered taking your mom's eyeliner pencil and drawing on a couple of armpit hairs, here are a few tips to make the wait for puberty more bearable.

> Actually, it was Emma L.'s mom's eyeliner. Wait, I mean... I don't know WHAT you're talking about! —Jenna

Bunk 9's
TOP THREE TIPS
for the BEST PUBERTY EVER!
(WHEN IT FEELS LIKE PUBERTY WILL NEVER COME)

1. OK, OK, we're repeating ourselves, but... Find someone older (and wiser) to talk to. Talking isn't just for girls already going through puberty. Even if you're still waiting for the first signs, you probably have questions, such as when it will happen, what will happen, and why it's not happening yet. Your mom, your best friend's mom, your older sister, your babysitter, your cousin, or Aunt Edna will be able to answer any questions you have, and reassure you that, yes, **IT WILL HAPPEN FOR YOU!** —EMMA L.

26

I have two dads and zero moms, but even
though they know everything, I wanted to talk
to a woman. When I was waiting and waiting
(and waiting) for puberty to start, our camp
counselor Julia helped reassure me that even
though I might not know WHEN it would happen,
it would absolutely, definitely happen. Eventually.
And it did. —Jenna

I wanted to know
EVERYTHING so I
asked EVERYONE.
—Brianna

2. **Enjoy the things you don't have to do.** Like not having to remember to bring an extra pad on a three-mile hike through the woods, finding a hidden spot to change that pad, and figuring out what to do with the old one. (Not that I know this from experience or anything!) —GRACE

3. **Learn from the mistakes of others.** If your friends have gotten a head start on puberty, it's hard not to feel left behind. But look at it this way: They're paving the way so your road will be smoother. From misadventures in hair removal to the mysteries of bra shopping, your friends' experiences can help you avoid any potential disasters of your own. —Abby

Abby's Tip for Extra-Late Bloomers

By the time puberty finally came around, it felt like I was the **last person on earth** to go through it. Every single one of my friends (and I mean every. single. one.) got their period before me. **Did I feel left out? YOU BET.** But I made sure to keep doing the things I loved—hip-hop classes, cooking, hanging out with my friends—and **not let it define me.** That way, when my boobs DID start growing, I was still Abby and not The Girl Who Went Through Puberty Last.

LEA'S GUIDE TO GOING GLOBAL

Those of us in Bunk 9 aren't the only ones excited for the road to womanhood. Did you know that across the world, different cultures have celebrations to mark becoming an adult? Here are a few of our favorites:

QUINCEAÑERA: This celebration of a girl's fifteenth birthday (the word comes from the Spanish words for "fifteen years") is now observed by many Mexican, Latin American, Caribbean, and Hispanic cultures. The lavish party originally marked the age at which a girl was ready to take on the responsibilities of adulthood, including marriage. Now it has evolved into a celebration of womanhood and community (though the party remains).

SEIJIN NO HI: This traditional Japanese ceremony is held annually on the second Monday of January and marks the new rights and responsibilities given to young adults who reached the age of twenty in the previous year.

BAT MITZVAH: In the Jewish tradition, the bat mitzvah, which literally means "daughter of commandments," happens at age twelve or thirteen (for boys it is a bar mitzvah at age thirteen). Often accompanied by a ritual celebration, it marks the age at which girls become women and members of the Jewish community and are responsible for following the commandments of Judaism.

RUMSPRINGA: Rumspringa is an Amish coming-of-age tradition that encourages young people to go out and experience the secular (nonreligious) world at the age of sixteen. Choosing to return to the Amish community marks a commitment to the Amish way of life.

PUBERTY JOURNAL

Part diary, part time line, all puberty! Use your puberty journal to record your feelings, write down the questions you have (and answers you receive!), list any tips you've discovered, and track the changes you're going through. Once you start your period, use it to track how long your period lasts, how heavy it is, and how often you get it. But more (much, much more) on that later!

Camp Silver Moon
WEEK 2

IN WHICH JENNA AND SAGE DISCOVER THAT **SOMETHING IS ROTTEN** IN THE STATE OF BUNK 9, AND EVERYONE ELSE IS GRATEFUL THEY'RE NOT THE OFFENDER.

Let's get one thing out of the way: Sage smelled.

And not in a roses-and-perfume sort of way. Sage smelled in an I-just-led-the-girls-to-victory-in-a-boys-against-girls-game-of-Capture-the-Flag sort of way. Which made sense, because she had.

Jenna was the one to point it out. We were all sitting around, still glowing from our big win and eating an evening snack of apples and peanut butter, when Jenna said, "GUYS, GUYS, GUYS, I DON'T KNOW WHO, BUT SOMEONE HERE REEKS." We all lifted our arms and gave our armpits a *good* sniff. Most of us were happy to confirm we weren't the offender. But Sage paused, and then leaned over to Jenna with her armpit still in the air and asked, "WAIT, is it me?" Jenna took in a deep whiff (rookie mistake) and then almost ran out of the room screaming.

After that, we all wanted to smell Sage's armpits. She was very obliging.

But still, it didn't exactly feel good to be told she smelled bad. And we understood—after all, IT COULD HAVE BEEN ANY OF US. Jenna and Grace didn't use deodorant, either. And Makayla had just started using it a month earlier.

Luckily, the next day, our counselor Julia gave Sage a present: **her very first stick of powder-fresh deodorant**. We admit it wasn't exactly the best present. But Julia also taught us all how to apply deodorant, and how to put on a shirt without getting white streaks on it, and how to stay smelling fresh if you don't want to use deodorant (Lea still doesn't use deodorant—she says it messes with her natural mojo). And that <u>was</u> the best present.

Sage wasn't the only one who learned something new that summer. Abby learned that she shouldn't brush her hair, and Brianna learned that she should. Emma R. learned how to shave her legs (and, a few years later, how to stop shaving them). Emma L. learned there was more than one use for baking soda, and we all learned the most important thing:

NO ONE WAKES UP KNOWING EXACTLY HOW TO BE A WOMAN, SO IT WAS A GOOD THING WE HAD EACH OTHER.

Walk around our bunk and you'll see personal hygiene products _everywhere_. (And if you're the camp inspector, we promise those products will be neatly organized any minute now!) Deodorant, zit cream, toothpaste, shampoo, conditioner, razors, face wash, hair gel, sunscreen, moisturizer, brushes, nail clippers...our list could go on and on and on.

WHY? Well, as you get older there's more you need to take care of. Some items, like toothbrushes and shampoo, have probably been part of your life for as long as you can remember. Other items, like DEODORANT and acne cream, may leave you scratching your head.

The good news is that other than a few essentials, almost everything else is optional. The better news is that once you know how everything works, personal hygiene (that's HI-jean, and it's the things you do to stay clean and healthy) feels less like a chore and more like a whole lot of FUN.

From the hair on your head to the jam between your toes **(ewwww)**, we'll tell you what's mandatory, what you can skip, and how to make the most out of everything that's available.

A VERY HAIRY SITUATION

Let's get one thing straight (or curly): There are some hair basics that are universal—HAIR SHOULD BE CLEAN!—but _everyone's hair is different_, which means everyone's hair needs different care. And if you're at Camp Silver Moon for the first time, it might also be your

first time caring for your hair entirely on your own. It takes some **trial and error** (and more error, and more trial, and a whole lot more error) to make your hair look its best, but we have a few tips and tricks to get you on your way. Don't forget, no matter how many errors you make, **your hair will ALWAYS grow back!**

STICK STRAIGHT

Straight hair tends to be naturally moisturized, which means *instant shine*. The downside? If you don't wash it often, that shine quickly turns to GREASE. And that grease will only get worse during puberty as your oil glands kick into high gear. Thanks, hormones! 😑

To keep your hair looking amazing, shampoo every one to two days. Use a light conditioner for a touch of extra silkiness (if you have thin, fine hair, use it only on the ends). Brush it in the morning and evening to keep it healthy and tangle-free, and you're good to go!

If you don't manage to yell "First!" on the way back to the bunk, a **hot** shower (emphasis on HOT) is hard to come by at Camp Silver Moon. My go-to low-maintenance hairstyle is a messy topknot.

Just flip your head upside down and gather your hair into a high ponytail in your hand. Then twist it all the way into a bun and loop a hair tie around it two or three times. If your hair is extra-long, you might need to tuck a few loose strands back into the hair tie. BONUS? This style works for medium to long hair—straight, wavy, or curly! —Jenna

Curls, Curls, Curls

Well-cared-for curls can be the envy of all of Bunk 9, but they take some wrangling and detangling. Curly hair is often more coarse, which means you need LESS shampoo and MORE conditioner.

Unless you spend all of Afternoon Swim lying with your head in the sand, SHAMPOO ONLY TWICE A WEEK. That will keep your hair from drying out. Use a heavy conditioner to add moisture every time you shower. If frizz isn't your thing, add a little product to define your curls. We like curl cream, gel, or mousse, but you'll have to experiment to find what's right for you. Most important, there are two absolute musts when it comes to curly hair: **Never, ever brush it when it's dry,** and always detangle it while it's wet.

Curly hair when brushed = Noooooooo!

If brushing is a big no-no, then how do you detangle? Apply conditioner in the shower, then run a comb through your hair (use a wide-tooth comb for tight curls, and a fine-tooth comb for loose curls). After your shower, flip your head and run your fingers through your hair to loosen the curls. Gently squeeze out any excess water with an old T-shirt (this will leave your hair less frizzy than a towel would). If you want, apply the product of your choice and... you're done! — EMMA L.

GOING NATURAL

One of the great things about natural black hair is that you have a million different hairstyles to choose from. Braids, twists, buns, curls, and all their variations mean you can sport a different look every day of camp. (OK, maybe not *every* day. You don't want to miss Lifeguard Training because you're styling your hair.)

Of course, well-styled hair means well-taken-care-of hair. Textured hair can get pretty dry, which means **MOISTURE IS KEY**. Instead of using shampoo, consider co-washing. Co-WHAT? Co-washing means using a special cleansing conditioner to clean your hair. Use it **ONCE A WEEK** the same way you would shampoo, and then condition every three to five days using a heavy conditioner. While you're conditioning, detangle your hair using a wide-tooth comb or your fingers, starting **from the ends and working your way to the roots,** and then rinse the conditioner out. Gently squeeze out any excess water with an old T-shirt, then apply a little styling product to help keep away the frizz. Look for ingredients such as argan oil, coconut oil, and shea butter in both your conditioner and your styling products.

If you don't want the rest of Bunk 9 yelling at you about the hot water, detangle with conditioner in your hair, but OUTSIDE the shower. Then jump back in to rinse, soap up, and go about your showery business! On days when you're not conditioning, use a shower cap to avoid rewetting your hair. And for super-easy summer styling, I top things off with a headband to match my mood! —Makayla

37

HEALTHY HAIR

The less heat and fewer chemicals you apply to your hair, the healthier and better looking it will be. That's true whether your hair is textured, curly, or straight. If your hair is textured, consider wearing it natural instead of relaxed (that is, chemically straightened). It will grow longer, look healthier, and break less. If your hair is currently relaxed and you want to switch to natural locks, you can either grow out the relaxed part and transition slowly, or take the plunge and cut it super short to start over. For girls with curls, waves, or straight locks, putting down the blow dryer, straightener, or curler will keep your hair from looking fried. No matter what kind of hair you have, wearing your own natural style means putting forward the best you!

Making Waves

Wavy hair is relatively *low maintenance.* If your hair falls on the straight side of wavy, you'll want to shampoo more often, use a very light conditioner, and brush morning and night. If your hair is thicker, shampoo every two or three days, use a medium to heavy conditioner, and detangle it with a comb while it's wet. Hair products are completely OPTIONAL, but on hot summer days, when Camp Silver Moon is unbearable anywhere but in the lake, a little bit of ANTI-FRIZZ PRODUCT will keep your hair looking perky while the rest of you wilts.

Brianna, remember when you didn't brush your hair for THREE WEEKS because your brush fell under the porch and you were scared you'd be attacked by a raccoon if you went to get it?
—Emma R.

Yup! And then my entire head was one big knot that took Julia two hours to detangle on the morning of Visiting Day.
—Brianna

CRISSCROSS (NO APPLESAUCE)

Short and medium-length hair may not be long enough for fancy updos, but that doesn't mean it has to lack style. Add a thick braid to one side and pull your hair into a low ponytail. Or braid two thin strands at the front of your face, and then pin them back for a perfect do for the Twelves-Thirteens Dance.

Kitchen Raid!

No, we're not suggesting you sneak into the dining hall kitchen for a midnight ice cream sandwich (take it from us—the walk-in freezer is kept locked at night), but we are suggesting you ask Leanne, the camp chef, for a few ingredients to whip up some homemade hair care!

Lea's Sea Salt Spray for
STRAIGHT & WAVY HAIR

Lake Silver Moon might leave your hair a bit... lake-y, but that doesn't mean your hair can't look like you spent the summer on the French Riviera. Use this spray on straight or wavy hair for a beachy bounce.

WHAT YOU NEED

1 spray bottle
1 cup warm water
1 tablespoon sea salt
1 tablespoon melted coconut oil
(running the jar under hot water should do the trick)

WHAT TO DO

In a spray bottle, combine the water, sea salt, and coconut oil and shake well. Spray onto slightly damp hair, flip your hair twice to loosen things up, and daydream about the South of France.

Emma L.'s Avocado Mask for
CURLY & NATURAL HAIR

If lunch was tuna casserole again, you might be tempted to eat this hair mask instead of putting it on your head, but when you feel how soft it leaves your curly or natural hair, you'll be happy you used it correctly.

WHAT YOU NEED

1 ripe avocado
1 ripe banana
2 large spoonfuls melted coconut oil
(running the jar under hot water should do the trick)

WHAT TO DO

Mash the avocado and banana together in a bowl, then add the coconut oil and mix well. Apply to dry or slightly damp hair, cover with a shower cap to avoid making a mess, and leave on for as long as you can stand it, or about thirty minutes. Shampoo (twice) to remove!

ITCHY & SCRATCHY

If you're having trouble keeping your hands off your scalp, talk to your counselor, your parents, the nurse, Emma R., or all of the above. It may be a case of dandruff—that is, a flaky scalp—in which case dandruff shampoo should do the trick. But it might also be... **LICE!** You'll need the help of an adult to get rid of lice, but you can prevent them. Don't share hairbrushes, headbands, hair ties, pillows, or hats, and keep your head a couple of inches away from your BFF's, even when whispering after Lights Out.

> Somehow I became the official Bunk 9 lice checker. Probably because I can spot a nit from a mile away!
> —Emma R.

OVER THE RAINBOW

Electric blue, **fire engine red**, cotton candy pink... while we believe in celebrating the natural us, it can be fun to change things up every once in a while, and nonpermanent (or semipermanent) hair dye is one way to experiment. It fades after a few weeks, which is great news if you discover *purple* is just not your color. Two important tips for dyeing hair: Always follow the allergy test instructions, and NEVER, ever dye your hair without getting your parents' permission.

> If you have dark hair like me, you may be disappointed to learn that the only thing non-permanent dye will color is your bathtub. —GRACE

> Thanks but no thanks— I like my hair just the way it is! —Jenna

PIZZA FACE!!!

Acne, pimple, zit, whitehead, blackhead, spot. The first blemish you see may be a sure sign that *puberty has arrived*. It may also make you want to scream. Our only words of comfort are that everyone—yes, EVERYONE—will see at least one pimple in their life, and many will see more, so you are not alone. But what exactly IS acne, and how in the world do you get rid of it???

> OK, so our counselor Julia told us that her second cousin's best friend's brother's girlfriend claims she has never had a pimple in her life, but we've never seen her, so we don't believe she actually exists.
> —Jenna

ACNE (The Basics)

Acne? More like ACK!-ne. (For the record, it's really pronounced AK-nee.) It's those sometimes-painful, often **GOO-FILLED BUMPS** that show up on your face starting in puberty. But what are they, exactly, and what causes them? **ACNE is an inflammation or swelling of the skin caused by clogged pores.** Your body always produces oil, but during puberty that oil production increases (thanks, hormones! 😑), and sometimes it's more than your pores can handle. Add bacteria that live on the skin to the mix, and you suddenly have clogged, swollen, red *pores* full of **EWWWW.**

> Pores? They're tiny holes in your skin that allow for the release of sweat and oils from your body. —Lea

42

WHAT'S BLACK AND WHITE AND RED ALL OVER?

(HINT: IT'S NOT A NEWSPAPER.)

The words **ACNE**, **PIMPLE**, and **ZIT** are all pretty interchangeable (and not fun), but most people think of **PIMPLES and ZITS** as blemishes that come out **one or two at a time**, and ACNE as blemishes that hang out in a group.

Because there's more than one kind of blemish, there's more than one way to get rid of them. So what's what, and how do you ATTACK A BREAKOUT?

BREAKING NEWS: YOU'RE BREAKING OUT!

BLACKHEADS: These are your most basic pimples, and they are so small you almost can't see them. When your pores get clogged and stay open, oil and bacteria react with the air and *turn black*. Blackheads are sometimes slightly raised, but mostly they're just visible as tiny black dots on your skin. Use a gentle face wash containing salicylic acid to keep your skin clean, and try adding a little over-the-counter acne spot treatment as well.

 If you don't have spot treatment handy, you can dab a mix of baking soda and water on whiteheads at night, which will help dry them out. —EMMA L.

<u>WHITEHEADS</u>: Almost as basic as blackheads, whiteheads happen when those same clogged pores close up. Whiteheads are raised white dots on your skin that are almost entirely on the surface, don't hurt, and aren't too swollen. They often appear around your *nose, chin, or forehead.* Use the same plan of attack as you would for blackheads.

<u>PAPULES & PUSTULES</u>: Now we're getting into acne territory. Papules are **HARD and RED**, and the skin around them is usually irritated. They often appear in groups, because they think your face is a party. Pustules are just like papules, but they're filled with PUS and appear white. Try treating both of these with **BENZOYL PEROXIDE OR SALICYLIC ACID.** However, if you're finding that they're not going away, you might want to talk to a dermatologist— that's a skin doctor—about other solutions.

<u>NODULES & CYSTS</u>: There's nothing to sugarcoat here—THESE ARE THE WORST. Nodules are big, angry pimples that go deep under the skin, are swollen, and hurt when you touch them. Cysts are their evil twins and are filled with **PUS.** Both are red and inflamed. If you have nodules or cysts, wash your face using a solution containing benzoyl peroxide, but you'll probably want to *visit a dermatologist,* who will help you come up with a plan of action, like trying to identify acne triggers and prescribing something you can't buy in the store.

> Sometimes outside factors irritate the skin and make your acne worse. For a while I was getting a ton of zits along my jawline. I started wearing my hair back, and while it didn't clear up completely, my skin definitely improved. Turns out oil from my hair was making my skin react!
> —Brianna

I got a mix of nodules and cysts on my cheeks starting when I was fourteen. I wish I could say they went away, but nope: I still have them! However, visiting a dermatologist definitely helped. She made some suggestions that I hadn't thought of, and while the acne is still there, it's a lot less severe than it was. Don't be embarrassed or afraid to ask for outside help. If we could fix acne on our own, dermatologists would be mostly out of a job. —GRACE

GET BACK!

We are sad to report that acne isn't limited to the face. Many people develop the dreaded <u>BACNE</u>, or back (also chest and shoulder) acne. So what can you do to help battle it?

* **Treat it the same way you would treat the acne on your face.** Use an acne wash on your back and shoulders when showering, and apply spot treatment to any visible zits. However, stay away from benzoyl peroxide spot treatments on bacne, as they will bleach your clothes, sheets, and pillowcase.

* **Go oil-free.** While you should never, ever skip sunscreen, sometimes it can clog your pores. Choose a sunscreen that's labeled "oil-free," "won't clog pores," or "dermatologist recommended."

* **Wash!** If you can, take a shower after exercising. Chances are there's sweat trapped in your clothing, building bacteria on your skin. But if you only have five minutes, wipe an acne pad over the breakout-prone area and change into a clean shirt.

* **Rinse!** Make sure to rinse off any remaining conditioner or other hair-product residue.

* **ROCK ON!** Confidence offsets pimples any day of the week. Wear tank tops and bathing suits with pride. After all, what's not to love about the skin you're in?!

INSIDE OUT?

Pimples are caused by _clogged pores_, but that doesn't mean that what's happening on the inside doesn't affect the outside. The jury is still out on exactly how stress and food affect your skin, but they're paying attention, and so should you.

If you've noticed that you seem to get a new zit every time you **THINK** about having to pass the Ropes Course Challenge, you're not alone. Many people seem to break out when they're stressed out, whether it's about an upcoming test or asking one of the Thirteens to the big dance.

You've probably heard that chocolate causes pimples too. And you've probably <u>also</u> heard that that's a big, giant myth. **SO WHICH IS IT!?**

There are foods that may trigger acne in individuals. Some popular offenders? SUGAR, DAIRY, AND NUTS. But don't swear off pistachio ice cream quite yet! What causes a breakout in one person might be perfectly fine for someone else. If you're worried that what you're eating is wreaking havoc on your skin, experiment with eliminating certain trigger foods, *one at a time*, for several weeks (at least three) to see if you notice an improvement. If nothing budges, feel free to keep eating them. We wouldn't want you giving up pistachio ice cream for nothing!

ON THE PROPER & IMPROPER
treatment of your face

PROPER: Wash your face two times a day. Use a fragrance-free, mild face cleanser, warm water, and clean hands. Just don't overdo it—natural oils are important for keeping your skin healthy. Too much washing will dry you out!

IMPROPER: Keep your mitts off your mug! The dirt and oils on your fingers can easily spread, so wash your hands before touching your face.

PROPER: Patience. The best way for that giant zit to disappear? On its own. It may be agonizing, but letting a pimple run its course will leave your skin happiest in the long run.

IMPROPER: Popping. We know you want to pop your pimples, but don't. Why? Popping your pimples can actually make the skin around them more inflamed, and breaking the skin leaves it open to more bacteria. In other words, it can make it much, much worse.

PROPER: Pop correctly. We know you're going to ignore our advice and pop anyway, so make sure you do it right and pop only whiteheads—that is, pimples that are entirely on the surface.

IMPROPER: Picking. What's worse than zits? Scars where your zits used to be. Which will definitely happen if you pick at them.

Yup! File that one under "learned the hard way." —Brianna

PROPER: Sharing. It's hard to know which face washes will work for you and which won't, especially when there are so many to choose from. Gather a small group of friends and trade face washes weekly until you all find ones you like. Just don't share any prescriptions you got from your doc.

IMPROPER: Giving up! Acne sucks. We know, because we have it (some more than others). But it doesn't define who you are! Make sure people can see the girl you are beneath your skin. The most important thing is having a happy and healthy lifestyle. And keep experimenting... you might find the perfect formula for you! Just know that eventually your skin will return <u>mostly</u> to normal.

Two summers ago, we (Jenna, Grace, and the Emmas) agreed to each bring a different face wash to camp and rotate once a week. It was great. Grace learned that salicylic acid wasn't quite strong enough for her, Emma R. learned to keep benzoyl peroxide away from her clothes, and we all got to try four times as many face washes as we would have otherwise! —EMMA L.

HOW TO POP A PIMPLE
(BUT THE CAMP NURSE DEFINITELY DOESN'T APPROVE)

First, wash your hands and face with warm water. Then very, VERY gently squeeze either side of the pimple until the insides release. Don't use your nails, and do NOT squeeze hard. If nothing budges, quit while you're ahead. Afterward, immediately rinse, dry, and coat with a dab of antibacterial ointment, benzoyl peroxide, or another pimple product. Just don't try this on pimples without a visible head or on those surrounded by red inflammation. They will only get bigger if you attempt to pop them.

CAN YOU HEAR ME?

Have you ever heard someone say, **"Never put anything smaller than your elbow in your ear?"** That's because trying to clean the wax out of your ears might actually cause more harm than good. A small amount of earwax helps protect your ears from bacteria, while Q-tips and other foreign objects can damage your eardrums. The good news is that your ears clean themselves. To get rid of any excess wax, wash your ears out gently with a washcloth. If you have any concerns, ask your doctor to take a look during your annual checkup.

THE HOLE SHEBANG

Pierced ears require special care so they don't get infected. If your ears are newly pierced, keep your earrings in for at least six weeks, rotating them a few times a day to help the holes heal properly. Give your ears a rinse with soap and water whenever you shower, and clean them twice a day by applying rubbing alcohol to the front and back of the hole using a cotton swab. If your ears have been pierced for a while, prevent infections by cleaning your earrings with rubbing alcohol before putting them in, and if your ears are sensitive to metals, stick to gold or surgical steel earrings. And remember, when it comes to piercing your ears, always get PERMISSION FROM YOUR PARENTS before taking the plunge, and NEVER, ever attempt to pierce them yourself. Leave the piercing to the pros.

SAY CHEESE!

Your smile is often the first thing people notice about you, so you'll want to keep your mouth healthy and clean. Brush your teeth for **two minutes, morning and night,** moving the head of your brush in a circular motion and making sure to get the front and back of every single tooth, including your molars. And don't forget to **BRUSH YOUR TONGUE** for super-clean breath! *Floss once a day* to remove any food that's stuck between your teeth and prevent bacteria from building up. Not only will it help you stay cavity free, but your bunkmates will appreciate your fresh breath when you're whispering after Lights Out!

Metal Mouth?

Brushing your teeth well when you have braces may take a little more effort, but it's also a lot more important. That's because food can easily get stuck around the braces, leading to bacteria, cavities, and bad breath. Choose a toothbrush with an angled head and carefully brush each tooth separately, making sure to completely clean around the braces. Don't forget the backs of your teeth and molars! And look for special floss that's made just for braces.

There's no getting around it—sometimes your breath is going to smell like the skunk that once sprayed Bunk 9. But what are some of the causes of HALITOSIS (that's hal-ih-TOE-sis, and it means bad breath), and **HOW DO YOU GET RID OF IT?**

MORNING BREATH: This is totally normal, everyday bad breath. During the day, saliva works to keep your mouth clean. At night, your mouth makes less saliva, allowing bacteria to come out and party. The fix? **Brush your teeth first thing in the morning.** By the time you eat something, freshness will be restored. —SAGE

GARLIC BREATH: You've probably noticed that when you eat certain foods, such as garlic or onions, your breath smells, uh, different. And not a good kind of different. But if, like me, there's no way you're skipping garlic bread night in the dining hall, sometimes you have to accept that bad breath comes with good eating. Try brushing your tongue as well as your teeth, drink plenty of water, and know that as long as you maintain good oral hygiene, your garlic breath will pass. —Emma R.

BAD-BRUSHING BREATH: The biggest cause of bad breath? BACTERIA. If you don't take care of your mouth, bits of old food in your teeth will rot and cause your breath to stink. Yup, totally gross. Also gross? I used to not brush my teeth at night. My dads would ask me if I'd brushed and I would nod and smile. Don't ask why—I have no idea. But three cavities (and one awful day when Grace's little brother told me my breath smelled like old garbage) later, I have fully embraced toothpaste, toothbrushes, and floss. —Jenna

51

IT'S THE PITS

Sad but true: Your armpits are probably going to get a little funky when you go through puberty. That's because your sweat glands— especially in your armpits, feet, and groin—go into overtime thanks to our new friends, HORMONES. 😑

It might seem like your armpits are wet all the time—and it doesn't help that when you're nervous (about making new friends, talking to your crush, passing the Ropes Course Challenge, or just about anything), **YOU SWEAT EVEN MORE.**

Sweat by itself doesn't smell, but when you combine sweat with the bacteria that occurs naturally on your skin, **things get STINKY Fast.** But that doesn't mean you can't keep your armpits smelling good, even in the middle of a competitive game of Capture the Flag!

If you find your shirts soaked through regularly, choose an antiperspirant, wear dark colors, or talk to your doc. Or rock out as usual and wear your sweat as a badge of honor— after all, *you're a woman now!* And don't worry, once you finish going through puberty, the sweat glands should calm down, at least a little bit.

THE NO-SMELL BASICS

1. **Keep things clean.** Shower regularly and don't be afraid to go to town on your pits with a bar of antibacterial soap. The less bacteria you have in your armpits, the less they'll smell.

2. **Dry off!** Bacteria grow best in warm, wet areas. Towel-dry your armpits thoroughly after your shower to minimize bacteria growth.

3. **Drink water.** Certain foods, such as garlic, onions, and even red meat, make you a bit stinkier. We'd never tell you to avoid eating these foods, but drinking water can help flush them through your system faster.

> Although if you care about animal rights, you might want to give up that red meat! —SAGE

4. **Wear natural fibers.** Fabrics like cotton allow your pits to breathe. More breathing equals less sweating, and less sweating equals less funk. Consider loose clothing as well, to avoid trapping the bacteria and moisture.

5. **Change your clothes daily.** When you smell bad, that smell transfers to your clothes and lingers, even if you shower. Wash your T-shirts after every wear to avoid reeking of yesterday's BO.

6. **Arm yourself** with the (optional!) deodorant of your choice, be it store-bought or homemade.

CALL FOR BACKUP!

(OR, CHOOSING THE RIGHT DEODORANT)

While we admit Lea's natural mojo smells great, if you're like the rest of us, you have a wide range of choices to help you eliminate your armpits' bacteria. Here's a breakdown:

As long as your scent isn't sending your bunkmates running, there's nothing wrong with the naturally scented you! —Lea

Antiperspirants reduce sweating while deodorants tackle odor. —Jenna

BUY: You can find deodorant in any drugstore or pharmacy, and many grocery stores too. Many girls opt for a deodorant-antiperspirant combo, which helps **combat both ODOR and SWEAT**. These come in stick, roll-on, and spray form. STICK deodorant is like a lip balm for your pits. Turn the dial at the bottom to raise the stick up far enough that the container doesn't scrape you, then swipe it over your armpits a few times. Roll-on deodorant is liquid and has a little ball at the top. Give your pits a little mini-massage, then do the chicken dance three times to get things dry. If you choose SPRAY, hold the can an inch away from your armpits and press down lightly. Just make sure you have the nozzle pointed toward your armpit! The downside to deodorant-antiperspirant? If you're looking for a natural option, this isn't for you. Check your local health food store for natural deodorants. They won't stop you from sweating, but they'll help with odor and make less of an environmental impact. —Makayla

Not all natural products are created equal. Check the ingredient list to make sure the one you choose really is natural—and that you're not allergic to anything. You may need to try a few out before you find one that works for you. —EMMA L.

You may have heard that antiperspirants, which contain aluminum, can contribute to getting cancer or Alzheimer's. The truth? There's no medical evidence to indicate that, so if you're not into sweating, feel free to apply antiperspirant liberally.

I learned the hard way: Don't stand too close to Jenna when she's applying spray deodorant. —GRACE

MAKE: I may have started my adventures in deodorant with a store-bought stick from Counselor Julia, but the truth is, I prefer to be natural. I'm not looking to re-create The Great Armpit Fiasco, but I want to make as little an impact as possible on my body and on the Earth. Sometimes I'll buy a natural stick at the health food store, but it's more fun to make deodorant at home. Ingredients such as **baking soda, coconut oil, olive oil, beeswax, shea butter, and essential oils** (like sage!) contain antibacterial properties and can be mixed together for a DIY deodorant. —SAGE

IMPROVISE: If you're in a pinch, try a pinch of **BAKING SODA**. It's used for baking, but it also helps *neutralize odors*. In fact, you might have an open box in your refrigerator, soaking up smells. Use your fingers or a clean cotton pad to brush baking soda onto clean, dry armpits. Just don't use the box from the fridge. —EMMA L.

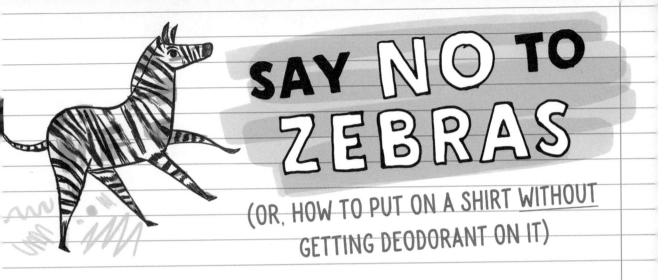

SAY NO TO ZEBRAS

(OR, HOW TO PUT ON A SHIRT WITHOUT GETTING DEODORANT ON IT)

If you use deodorant regularly, chances are you also regularly get white marks all over your shirt. But if you want to expand your fashion choices beyond animal prints or solid white T-shirts, here's a quick how-to on staying streak-free.

1. Put your head through the neck hole of your shirt, keeping both the sleeves and the body of the shirt above your shoulders and away from your armpits.

2. Use one arm to hold the shirt as far away from your pits as possible while you slip your other arm into the sleeve, unrolling the shirt over your arm and body at the same time.

3. Pull the shirt down over the other half of your body, while carefully slipping your other arm into the other sleeve.

4. Breathe.

Streak-free shirts belong in the Advanced Deodorant Wear category. If you find yourself with white stuff on your shirt, try rubbing the fabric together to get the stain out.
—Abby

Head, Shoulders, Pits, and Toes. (PITS AND TOES!)

We keep talking about getting clean, but how often do you really need to shower? The answer is as murky as Lake Silver Moon. If you spend most of your time kicking butt in volleyball, you'll probably want to shower every day or two. If not, there's nothing wrong with jumping in the shower every three days. Too much showering strips your skin of its natural oils, and can leave you dry and cracked. On the days you do get in, use a mild soap to get clean, spending the most time on your armpits, butt, and groin, and resist the urge to drain ALL the hot water.

THE SKIN YOU'RE IN

Your skin is your largest organ, so it should come as no surprise that it needs some care. Most important? **PROTECT IT.** Regularly wear **SUNSCREEN with an SPF OF 15 or GREATER** (make that SPF 30 if you're particularly prone to burning), no matter what your skin tone is, anytime you're outside. Make sure to *reapply it* every couple of hours and after you swim. And if you're heading down to Lake Silver Moon, throw on a caftan—or at least a baseball cap—for extra protection. And borrow a beach umbrella from the waterfront shed!

I burn just by THINKING about the sun, so it's caftans, big hats, and plenty of sunscreen for me. I apply sunscreen before going out, then reapply it every hour, or after swimming. —Jenna

If you're going to be lying in the sand, don't forget to lather up the bottom of your feet. —Makayla

GIVE ME A HAND

Your hands are two of your most important tools of communication. After all, you use them to wave hello, make friendship bracelets, and pass notes during Morning Meeting. Unfortunately, you also use them to pass bacteria to other people, so it's important to **KEEP THEM CLEAN**. You probably already know you should wash your hands with soap after you use the bathroom, but did you know you should also wash them after finishing your morning chores, petting the camp dog, visiting your best friend in the infirmary, or when you have Kitchen Patrol? Always wash your hands for twenty seconds or more, using warm water and soap.

You Nailed It!

There are two steps to beautiful, healthy nails: Clean and cut them. Keeping your nails clean keeps bacteria from building up, but it also makes them look good! Use a nailbrush and warm, soapy water to scrub underneath your nails and get rid of any dirt. Once you've given your nails **a GOOD soaking**, use either nail clippers or nail scissors to carefully trim them (the water will soften them, making them easier to cut). The same goes for the nails on your toes!

An optional third step for beautiful nails? Polish! Apply nail polish from the base of your nail toward the tip. Don't worry about making it perfect. Once the polish is fully dry, you can rub any extra polish off your fingers after soaking them in the shower. Just don't use up all the hot water! —GRACE

This Bites!

When you spend your days working in the camp garden, playing Capture the Flag, and crossing the dreaded Ropes Course, your hands are bound to get dirty. And when you put those hands in your mouth, you're giving the day's bacteria free access to your insides. Which means when it comes to nail-biting moments, **JUST SAY NO!**

Confessions of a Former Nail Biter
(OR HOW TO KICK THE HABIT IN FIVE REALLY DIFFICULT STEPS) by Abby

Until I was fourteen, my nails practically DIDN'T EXIST—that's how much I bit them. But that summer we had a bout of pinworms going around the bunk (I know. SO GROSS. I'm still traumatized!), and I was determined to stop biting my nails. A combination of the strategies on the next page did the trick, and now I'm first in line for a manicure when Bunk 9 decides to have a spa day.

1. **Wear bright nail polish.** Chances are, you don't even notice your fingers as they are approaching your mouth. If you paint your nails in a bright color, such as red or green, you're bound to see them before it's too late.

2. **Coat your nails with anti-nail-biting polish.** Yup, this stuff tastes terrible. Which is why it works! Put it on top of your regular nail polish for an added barrier. Just try not to get any in your eyes.

3. **Enlist your friends.** Brianna and Makayla were tasked with <u>lightly</u> smacking my hands out of my mouth any time they saw me trying to bite my nails. They might have had a bit more fun than they needed to with that assignment!

> Bonus! This stuff also works for thumb sucking. I mean, if that's something you need.
> —Jenna

4. **Cover your nails.** When steps one through three aren't doing the trick, head down to Arts & Crafts and put decorative tape over your nails. You can either wrap it around your fingers or cut pieces in the shape of your nails.

5. **Look for your triggers.** If you notice that you bite your nails when you're nervous or when you're bored, try to find something else that will get you through those times.

6. **Cut yourself some slack.** Trust me, it's not easy to stop biting your nails. If at first you don't succeed, just try again!

Under-WHERE???

OK, we know the main reason you're reading The Book is to get to the **PERIOD** part! But while we solemnly swear to give you the whole truth about periods and other mysteries of the vagina, first we need to talk about hygiene.

Guess what? **The vagina is SELF-CLEANING!!!!** Seriously: It. Cleans. Itself. The vagina produces secretions called DISCHARGE (one of the mysteries we'll cover later), which serve to keep the inside of your vagina clean. Not only that, but the bacteria that live in your vagina are the good kind of bacteria—they're working hard to make sure you stay infection-free. In fact, cleaning your vagina too much can actually LEAD to infection.

The best way to keep your vagina healthy is to leave it mostly as is (after all, it's perfect). Every time you shower, using your hand or a washcloth, wash the outside with warm water and, if you want, a little bit of gentle, unscented soap. You don't need to clean the inside—it's doing that all by itself!

While the inside of your vagina is full of good bacteria, bad bacteria can easily find their way to the party. KEEP THE AREA CLEAN: Make sure to dry off with a towel after showering, wear cotton underwear to allow for plenty of air flow, and change your underwear daily so that you're not sitting in yesterday's sweat and discharge (because EWWWW). —GRACE

HAIR TODAY, MORE TOMORROW

Have you ever heard the expression "Hair today, gone tomorrow"? We're not totally sure what it means, but when you're going through puberty, it probably feels like **THE EXACT OPPOSITE IS TRUE.**

Not only is hair sprouting in places it never was before—hello, underarms, upper lip, belly button, and pubic region—but your leg hair is most likely getting thicker and more noticeable as well. So what options do you have when it comes to your NEW FUZZ?

1. **DO NOTHING.** Hair is a natural part of becoming an adult. Everyone grows hair when they go through puberty, so embrace it as a new adventure, wear it as a badge of honor, dye your armpits if you want, and go about your day! We know it's not the most conventional choice, but then again, you're not the most conventional girl. And if anyone tells you otherwise, just throw The Book at them.

Did we say dye your armpits? Yup! If you choose to keep your armpit hair, why not have a little fun and dye it blue, pink, green, or any color you want? Just ask your parent or guardian for permission first, of course! —SAGE

2. REMOVE IT. We get it: Change can be weird, and hair in new places is definitely a change. If you don't like your leg or armpit hair, you should feel free to get rid of it. We'll give you the A-to-Z's of hair removal so you can do it safely. Just remember, you should remove your hair only if _you_ want to. If anyone else tells you to remove your body hair, throw The Book at them!

3. REMOVE <u>SOME</u> OF IT. No one said body hair had to be all or none. You can wax your legs but not your armpits; you can shave your armpits but not your legs; you can do all of it sometimes and none of it other times. After all, it's your body and your body hair—do what feels right to you. And if anyone disagrees, throw The Book at them!

pubic speaking

If you find that your pubic hair extends past the line of your bathing suit, you can choose to wax or shave the part that sticks out—like coloring inside the lines. Then again, some of us had the most fun when we went freestyle in our coloring books, so the choice to remove some pubic hair is entirely your own.

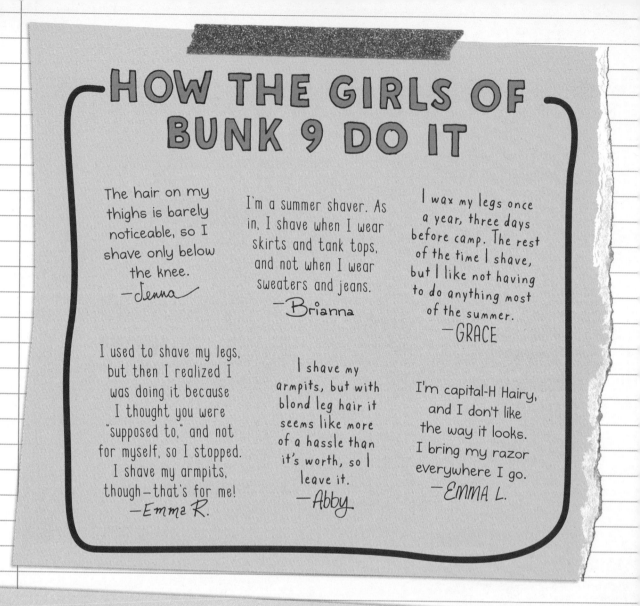

HOW THE GIRLS OF BUNK 9 DO IT

The hair on my thighs is barely noticeable, so I shave only below the knee.
—Jenna

I'm a summer shaver. As in, I shave when I wear skirts and tank tops, and not when I wear sweaters and jeans.
—Brianna

I wax my legs once a year, three days before camp. The rest of the time I shave, but I like not having to do anything most of the summer.
—GRACE

I used to shave my legs, but then I realized I was doing it because I thought you were "supposed to," and not for myself, so I stopped. I shave my armpits, though—that's for me!
—Emma R.

I shave my armpits, but with blond leg hair it seems like more of a hassle than it's worth, so I leave it.
—Abby

I'm capital-H Hairy, and I don't like the way it looks. I bring my razor everywhere I go.
—EMMA L.

While there's no real health risk in removing your leg or armpit hair, the sensitive skin around your pubic area is more susceptible to nicks, cuts, and irritation when shaved or waxed. Combine that with your natural bacteria, and infection can result. Not only that, but just like your eyelashes and nose hairs help protect your eyes and nose from foreign objects, your pubic hair can help protect your vagina from bad bacteria by forming a barrier.

If you do decide to remove some pubic hair, stick to your bikini line (the hair that goes beyond your bathing suit), and let the rest of it work its magic!

THE A-TO-Z'S OF REMOVING BODY HAIR

SAY WHAT?

SAY HOW?

shaving

Sitting in or on the edge of a bathtub, or on a towel on the floor, apply shaving cream to your skin. Using a very light amount of pressure, run the razor over your skin in smooth, careful strokes, against the direction of hair growth (on legs, start at your ankles and move up). Rinse the razor between strokes to clean out any hair and shaving cream. Dry off, then apply body lotion. If after some time your razor isn't quite doing its job, it might be time to change the blade.

waxing

Hot wax is applied and removed—along with your hair. Depending on how brave you are, you can do this at home, but we recommend going to a pro, at least the first few times. You <u>don't</u> want to get burned.

depilatory cream

This is a cream that dissolves hair where it meets your skin. Apply to the area of hair you'd like to remove, wait the amount of time stated on the box (usually about three to five minutes), and rinse off well.

If you make the choice to remove some or all of your body hair, doing it with the right tools will make a world of difference. Most women choose to shave, wax, or use a hair-removal cream. Just remember: Before removing any hair anywhere on your body, always talk to a parent or guardian.

SAY YAY? SAY NAY?

Shaving is pain-free, and you can make it part of your shower routine.

Because it only cuts the hair off at the skin's surface, you'll find your hair growing back pretty quickly. Chances are, if you decide to shave you'll need to do it every one to two days. And remember, light pressure! If you press down too hard, you run the risk of cutting yourself. If you accidently nick yourself, rinse the cut with water and soap, dry it, and apply pressure with a washcloth or tissue until the bleeding stops.

Waxing pulls hair up from the roots, so you need to do it only about once a month.

Waxing pulls hair out from the roots, so OUCH.

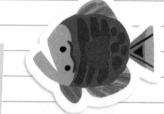

Hair-removal cream is easy and pretty pain-free. It also lasts a bit longer than shaving—about three to five days.

If your skin is sensitive, you might find that the cream burns or that you have an allergic reaction. Depilatory cream also works best on fine hair, so if your hair is coarse, you might need to use it more often or try a different method. And if you prefer using natural products, this one probably isn't for you.

THINGS THAT GO BUMP

Many people get red, itchy bumps called *razor burn* from removing hair. (Yes, it's called razor burn even if you wax or use a cream.) If in the days after shaving you can't stop scratching, APPLY ALOE VERA or a topical gel meant to relieve razor burn. To avoid razor burn altogether, try using an antibacterial aftershave gel or lotion. Another cause of bumps? INGROWN HAIRS. These are hairs that grow back into the skin rather than coming out through your pores. The result is a painful bump that often looks like a small pimple. To get rid of them, apply a warm washcloth to the area for a few minutes to open up the pore, and use a gentle exfoliating soap and tweezers to ease the hair back out.

PLAYING FOOTSIE

FEET STINK. OK, not all feet stink, but if you just played Capture the Flag in sneakers without socks, chances are that yours do. Why? Feet have the same sort of *sweat glands* that are in your armpits and groin,

which means that when puberty hits, they get sweaty, and then smelly when they mix with bacteria. To keep your bunkmates from tossing all of your shoes onto the back porch with the raccoons, always pair closed-toed shoes with clean cotton socks, QUICKLY CHANGE OUT OF WET OR SWEATY SOCKS, and give your feet and toes *a good scrub* whenever you shower, remembering to dry them off well.

When my feet get particularly stinky, I wash them with three tablespoons of apple cider vinegar. Gross? Maybe. Effective? 100 percent. —SAGE

IT'S PERSONAL!

We all know sharing is caring, but when it comes to personal hygiene, it's best to keep things, well, personal. Toothbrushes, deodorant, and even bar soap keep you clean by removing bacteria. When you share them with your bunkmates, you're effectively passing your bacteria back and forth to each other. Which, EWWWW.

A good rule of thumb is not to share anything that makes DIRECT CONTACT WITH YOUR SKIN. That includes nail clippers, razors, stick deodorant, and towels. And don't ever share prescription medicines. As for shampoo, hair gel, face wash, spray deodorant, and other items that are protected by a bottle, feel free to borrow them freely. Just make sure you ask first!

Camp Silver Moon
WEEK 3

IN WHICH GRACE STUFFS HER BRA WITH DISASTROUS RESULTS, AND **THE SILVER MOON SISTERHOOD IS FORMED.**

That summer, we thought about nothing but BREASTS. OK, that's not totally true—we also thought about our upcoming dance with the Thirteens, the tree house our bunk was building, and the family of raccoons that woke us up each night—but BOOBS WERE ON ALL OF OUR MINDS. A LOT.

Brianna and Makayla had them the summer before, but now all of a sudden they were B-I-G big. Emma R. had them too, but she'd had them for so long, none of us paid any attention, least of all her. Emma L. had ONE (and only one). And Jenna and Grace spent hours scanning their chests in the full-length mirror in the counselor area for any signs of growth. (An ocean away, Lea was staring into her own mirror, desperately waiting for something to happen.) Only Sage, who had mosquito-bite bumps, and Abby, who didn't, were too busy to notice. And then Grace had the BRILLIANT IDEA to BORROW one of Emma L.'s bras. AND STUFF IT. It took six tissues on each side to fill.

Everything was fine—though a bit LUMPY—during Arts & Crafts and Music Under the Big Tree. EVERYTHING WAS LESS FINE DURING SPORTS. If we hadn't been playing volleyball, maybe all would have been OK. But we were, and Grace is AWESOME at volleyball. So when she went to spike the ball, she did not hold back. The combination of jumping and swinging her arm was not good. **The tissues in the left side of her bra CAME FLYING OUT** of the top of her tank top. All six of them. And while they did not go over the net, they still somehow landed on the other side. Let's just say that Grace spent a lot of time that summer being asked if she had a tissue.

One super-fabulous thing did come out of THE GREAT TISSUE DISASTER: That night after Lights Out, we sat in a big circle in the center of our bunk and comforted Grace. We promised that through big boobs and small boobs, we would stick together.

AFTER ALL, WE WERE

BOSOM BUDDIES.
BREAST FRIENDS.

WE WERE, FROM THAT MOMENT ON, THE

SILVER MOON SISTERHOOD.

the Boobs of Bunk 9!

These are the boobs of Bunk 9: big, little, pointy, round, flat, pear-shaped, high, low, firm, mushy, perky, saggy. Yup, just like the people who are attached to them, **our breasts are as UNIQUE as snowflakes**.

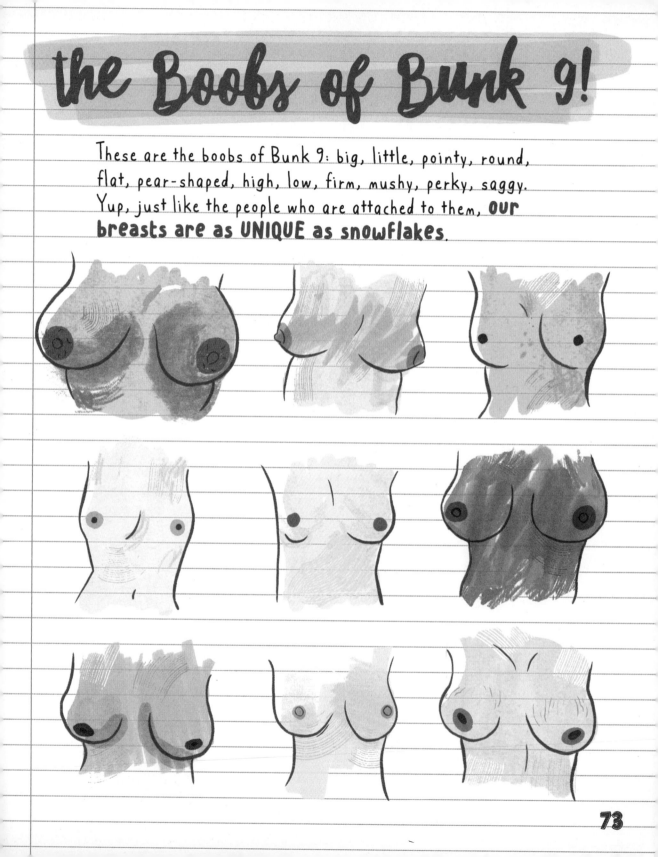

OK, it's true that we haven't done an in-depth examination of ALL the boobs of the world, but has anyone seen every snowflake that ever fell, either? Exactly.

Look around and you'll see breasts in an endless variety of shapes and sizes. In fact, check out your own set. Chances are, you'll even see tiny differences between your two breasts. But whether you're still waiting for the first signs of growth or you've been expertly wearing a bra for years, one thing is true: **All members of the Silver Moon Sisterhood (including you) either have them or will get them!**

WHAT ARE BREASTS? (THE BASICS)

Breasts, also known as boobs, TITS, JUGS, and (our personal favorite) GAZONGAS, are those two mounds on your mom's chest, your aunt Edna's chest, and—soon—on your chest. Scientifically speaking, the main function of breasts is to produce milk when you have a baby. They're part of the package that signifies that your body is ready to have a child. Not scientifically speaking (because, let's be honest, having a baby is probably fifteen to INFINITY years away), breasts are one way to tell men and women apart, they're fun to squeeze when you're sitting alone on your bunk bed, and they look good in a variety of outfits.

WHAT ARE BREASTS? (THE INS & OUTS)

On the inside, the human breast is made of a mix of tissues—no, not _that_ kind of tissue, but the kind of tissue that our entire body is made up of. Breasts are composed of glandular tissues that make milk (but don't worry, your breasts won't have milk in them until you have a baby) and fatty tissues that determine how big your breasts will get.

On the outside, you'll see a darker circle near the middle of your breast called the _areola_ (that's AIR-ee-OH-la), and in the center of the areola, you'll see the NIPPLE.

> It may be called fatty tissue, but your weight has only a little to do with your breast size.
> —EMMA L.

The Circle Game

Did you know that areolas can be **BIG** or **SMALL** or **IN-BETWEEN**? They're usually darker than the rest of the breast, but we've seen areolas that are almost the same color as the breast itself. They can range in color from very LIGHT PINK to very DARK BROWN. Sometimes the areola is a defined circle. Sometimes the edges are so soft they seem to blend into the breast.

The nipple can be big or small too; it can _stand out_ like a pencil eraser or **lie soft** against the areola. Sometimes nipples are even inverted (that means they poke in instead of out). There's just NO WRONG WAY for nipples and areolas to be!

WHAT'S THIS WHOLE PROCESS GOING TO LOOK LIKE?!?

ONE THING'S FOR SURE:

You're not going to go from THIS

to THIS overnight.

So you don't need to worry about heading to the dining hall tomorrow morning with a brand-new body.

Most girls start developing breasts sometime between *the ages of nine and fourteen*, but it can start earlier or later. It usually takes about **THREE TO FIVE YEARS** from when your breasts start developing until they fully stop growing. During this time, your breasts will go through FIVE STAGES. You may notice all of them, but sometimes the changes are so subtle, you might think you've skipped a stage.

I had boobs at age eight. —Emma R.

And I had almost nothing until this year. —Abby

76

1. The NO-boob. This is what you look like before you start puberty. You probably recognize it from the first several years of your life.

2. The BUDDING boob. The first thing you'll notice when your breasts start to develop is a bump about the size of a nickel or quarter underneath your nipple. This is called a breast bud. It's usually hard, and sometimes a little painful to touch. You might get only one breast bud at first, but don't worry, eventually you'll get the other. It's perfectly normal for one boob to develop before the other, but they'll (mostly) even out. During this phase, your areolas might also get a little bigger and darker.

3. The GROWING boob. This is the exciting part! During this stage your boobs will continue to grow (and possibly grow, and grow, and grow). You're developing that tissue we talked about earlier.

4. The FINISHING boob. Your areolas and nipples will continue to grow and darken. They may appear puffy and might look like an entirely separate mound on top of your breast. They may even grow a few hairs! You can (carefully) snip or tweeze these, but feel free to leave them be.

5. The BOOB boob! Your breasts will round out and meet up with the areolas and nipples so that they no longer seem separate. These are your breasts! Don't you just love them?

EMMA R.'S NOTE FOR EARLY BIRDS

One of the best things about womanhood is sharing your experiences with other women, but that's not so easy to do if you're the first! Find someone older and wiser to confide in—your mom or sister, your aunt Edna, a babysitter, or your cousin. They can give you tips until your friends catch up. (Don't worry, soon you'll be the one giving out tips!) And for the girls of Bunk 9: Camp counselors are especially good at doling out womanly advice.

JUST HOW BIG WILL THEY GET?

We checked our Magic 8 Ball, and it said, "ASK AGAIN LATER." It's almost impossible to know how big your boobs will get, but your genes might help point you in the right direction. Take a look at your mom and your aunt Edna. Their boobs might hold the secret to yours. But don't forget, genetics come from both your mom and your dad, and there's no telling which side of the family you'll take after. You might even get your body type from a distant relative a few generations back. Starting your development **EARLY or LATE won't determine your size**, either. Our big tip here: Be patient and eventually you'll know!

Bust Creams, Chants, and Pills:
DO THEY WORK?

If you have not read Judy Blume's <u>Are You There God? It's Me, Margaret</u>, then please put The Book down immediately, **RUN**—don't walk—to the camp library, and read it cover to cover. We'll wait right here.

Done? OK then. So now when we say, "We must, we must, we must increase our bust!" you'll know what we're talking about. But do all of those bust exercises, enhancement creams, and enlargement pills actually work? As Jenna can tell you, THEY DO NOT. Not only that, but the safety of creams and pills isn't fully known, and you could potentially be putting something harmful in or on your body. Skip them. After all, your boobs are perfect just as they are! As for exercises? They won't help make your boobs bigger either, but no one will stop you from exercising for the fun of it!

Yup, I don't like to admit it, but I definitely spent the better part of my fourteenth year rubbing enhancement cream into my boobs. That's $75 of babysitting money I could have spent going to the movies. Now I've embraced my small boobs by wearing strapless and backless dresses whenever possible. No bra required! —Jenna

CaN i shRiNk THEM?

We love our big boobs, and so should you! But we get it—sometimes they're a literal pain in the bust, especially when it comes to sports. You can't give your boobs back (and why would you want to?), but a good sports bra or underwire bra can do wonders. Look for bras with a lot of support (more on that later) to help keep everything in place while you work toward running that five-minute mile.

PROPER KEEPING OF BREASTS
for Proper (and Improper) Ladies

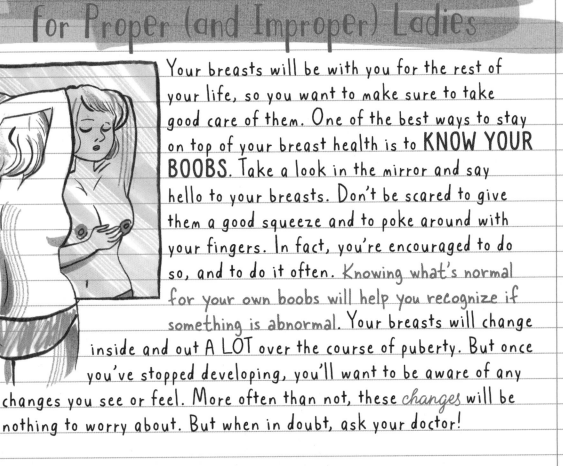

Your breasts will be with you for the rest of your life, so you want to make sure to take good care of them. One of the best ways to stay on top of your breast health is to **KNOW YOUR BOOBS.** Take a look in the mirror and say hello to your breasts. Don't be scared to give them a good squeeze and to poke around with your fingers. In fact, you're encouraged to do so, and to do it often. Knowing what's normal for your own boobs will help you recognize if something is abnormal. Your breasts will change inside and out A LOT over the course of puberty. But once you've stopped developing, you'll want to be aware of any changes you see or feel. More often than not, these changes will be nothing to worry about. But when in doubt, ask your doctor!

WANT TO SKIP THE LONG LINE AT THE CAMP INFIRMARY?

Here are a few things that are and are not perfectly normal.

POTENTIAL PROBLEM	NORMAL OR NOT?	POTENTIAL SOLUTION
BREASTS FEEL TENDER OR SWOLLEN	Probably normal! Are you about to start your period? If so, tender or swollen breasts may be a symptom of PMS (premenstrual syndrome). And remember, growing pains apply to boobs too, so don't freak out if they hurt while they're still developing.	Wait a few weeks and see if the tenderness goes away. If you're still in pain a week after your period, talk to your doctor.
BUMPY AREOLAS	Totally normal! In fact, almost everyone has bumps on their areolas. These are glands that secrete a tiny amount of oil to keep your areolas from getting dry.	No solution needed! More important: No solution should be taken. These are not zits, so resist any urge to pop them, especially as trying to do so could cause infection.
HAIRY AREOLAS	Totally normal! Yup, it's true, as we develop, we might grow some hair on our areolas.	Probably nothing! If you want, you can very carefully pluck the hair, but you absolutely don't have to. If you can count the number of hairs, there's nothing to worry about. But if you suddenly grow a lot more hair than you've had before, you might check in with your doctor.
INVERTED NIPPLES	Totally normal! Sometimes nipples go in instead of out. This is called inverted nipples.	Absolutely nothing! But if your nipples have always poked out and they suddenly get shy and retreat, talk to your doc.
NIPPLE DISCHARGE OR SECRETION	Potentially abnormal, but not necessarily. If you've just given your nipple a good pinch or squeeze and you notice a little bit of discharge, you have no reason to worry.	If your nipples start releasing discharge without any stimulation, you should have it checked out. And if you have bloody discharge, always get it looked at by a doctor.

POTENTIAL PROBLEM	NORMAL OR NOT	POTENTIAL SOLUTION
LUMPS ON THE INSIDE	Probably normal, especially if you're just starting to develop. You might be feeling your breast bud, which is often hard and lies underneath the nipple. If your boobs are fully developed, most likely you're feeling breast tissue you haven't noticed before.	If you feel a hard lump that wasn't previously there, ask your doctor to check it out. They'll most likely confirm it's nothing, but it's important to get it looked at. And remember, the better you know your boobs, the better you'll know what's normal for you!
STRETCH MARKS	Totally normal! If you have a sudden growth spurt in your breasts (or hips, or thighs, or butt), you may notice small stretch lines on your skin.	None needed! The marks will probably fade on their own. But if you feel like experimenting, try rubbing a little olive oil, cocoa butter, or even egg whites (ewwww!) into your skin every day for a month. Then again, if you don't feel like turning yourself into a human salad, you can do nothing at all.
ONE BOOB IS BIGGER THAN THE OTHER	Totally normal! When you first start developing, one breast often grows before or faster than the other. Eventually your other boob will (mostly) catch up. But they might never be exactly the same size—most women have one breast that is slightly larger.	Be patient and they'll even out. Chances are the difference is only noticeable to you anyway. But if the difference is more than a cup size, try buying a padded bra with removable padding, which you remove from only one side.
UPPER-BODY PAIN FROM BOOBS	Unfortunately, normal if you have extra-large boobs. Sometimes if breasts are really big, the added weight can cause back and shoulder pain.	A really supportive bra can be a huge help. But while we hope you love your big boobs, if you're constantly in pain, we get it if you don't. If a good bra doesn't do the trick, talk to your doctor. A breast reduction (meaning surgery to make them smaller) might be an option when you've stopped growing.
TOUCHING YOUR BREASTS MAKES YOU FEEL TINGLY AND GOOD INSIDE	Totally and completely normal! Your breasts are an erogenous zone (that's eh-RAW-jen-us). That means when they're touched, they might make you feel good. Not everyone's breasts are sensitive, but if yours are, that's a definite bonus!	If touching your boobs makes you feel good, then by all means keep touching them! We just recommend doing it in the privacy of your own room or bathroom (not in the middle of Bunk 9!).

THE ABC'S AND 123'S OF BRAS

Now that we've talked breasts, let's talk bras. Buying a bra can be confusing. First there are all of those numbers and letters that practically require a college degree to understand. Then there are a billion and a half different types of bras to choose from. Triangle? Sports? Underwire? **WHAT DOES IT ALL MEAN?!**

WHAT IS A BRA?

Booby trap, boob sling, over the shoulder boulder holder. In other words, a bra, or brassiere, is that piece of clothing you've seen your mom and your aunt Edna wear under their clothes.

Scientifically speaking, **it holds the boobs in place**, and sometimes shapes them. Not scientifically speaking, bras can present a chance to privately experiment with **different fashion personalities.**

DO I HAVE TO WEAR A BRA?

<u>NO.</u> THERE IS NO MEDICAL REASON TO WEAR A BRA. Some women wear a bra because they find it uncomfortable when their boobs move around if they go braless or because a bra gives them the shape they want. Other women don't like the feeling of their clothes rubbing against their nipples. But there are women who don't like the feeling of a bra strap against their skin or find bras constricting. While most women choose to wear a bra once they start going through puberty, it is strictly a fashion choice—one that's entirely yours to make!

> I wore a bra for six months because I wanted to see what the big deal was, but I love how free my boobs feel when I don't wear one. Now I only wear a bra when I run. And I get to sleep an extra two minutes while everyone else gets dressed. —SAGE

> I WISH I could go braless! But my boobs are so big that without a bra they just feel totally out of control. Thanks, but I'll opt for the harness! —Brianna

84

Sizing Things Up

Bras come in sizes that are a mix of numbers and letters, such as 34A or 36D. The number refers to how big around your rib cage is, and the letter (or letters) refers to the size of the breasts themselves. Figuring out your bra size is one of the most confusing things about being a woman. (Once you've mastered this, everything else should be smooth sailing.) Luckily, there's a very specific formula to help MAKE THINGS A LITTLE EASIER. Ready? Let's go!

1. Using a soft tape measure, measure all the way around your rib cage, right underneath your boobs. You'll want the tape measure to sit snugly against your skin. Round to the nearest inch. If the number is odd, add five; if even, add four. This is your BAND NUMBER, so write it down.

$$\begin{array}{r} 29 \\ +5 \\ \hline 34 \end{array}$$

37

2. Now measure around your back and across the fullest part of your breasts (usually across the nipples). This time the tape measure can be a *little bit looser*—you don't want to feel like you're squishing your boobs! **Round to the nearest number.** This is your **bust measurement.** Write this number down too.

3. Time for math! **Subtract your band number from your bust measurement.** Now use this number to determine your cup size.

Less than 1 = AA   3 = C
1 = A   4 = D
2 = B   5 = DD

Put it all together. Your band number and cup size together make your bra size. So your bra size is a **34C.**

$$29 + 5 = 34$$

$$37 - 34 = 3 \rightarrow C$$

34C!

Still confused? Us too! The best way to find a bra that fits and is comfortable is to try on several bras in different sizes and from different brands. You'll want the band to fit around snugly but not tightly (you should be able to breathe!). Your **BOOBS SHOULD FILL THE CUP** completely. If your boobs are getting flattened, try going up a size. If the fabric is gaping on the sides, try a smaller cup size. Your boobs are like snowflakes, so some brands will naturally fit better than others. And remember, if all of this makes you scream, "Je ne comprends pas!" (that's French for "I DON'T UNDERSTAND!"), you can always go braless.

Most bra stores and lingerie departments (that's lon-jer-AY, and it refers to bras and underwear) have sales associates who will measure you for free. Let yourself be pampered and get fitted by a pro. —Brianna

Bras stretch over time, so if you choose a bra with multiple hooks, you'll want it to fit on the loosest one when you first buy it. After some time, switch to the middle hook, and eventually to the tightest. —Emma R.

OODLES OF BOOBIES:
CHOOSING THE RIGHT BRA (OR NOT) FOR YOU

Bra shopping can be overwhelming. (We've broken down in tears more than once in the middle of a department store.) So it's best to buddy up, especially if you're buying **YOUR FIRST BRA**. Ask your mom, or your best friend who has already been there, to go with you. They'll be able to help point you in the right direction—and steer you away from the wrong one!

Do you want to go bra shopping with me? —Jenna

Do I want to? It's my duty! How else can I stop you from buying a water bra? —Makayla

87

If you're not sure which of the *millions* (not actually) of bra types is right for you, you can always try them all. But if spending the next **forty years** bra shopping wasn't on your to-do list, use the chart below to help narrow your choices.

WHAT IT DOES 　　　 WHO IT'S FOR

BRALETTE

WHAT IT DOES: A hybrid between a bra and a tank top, a bralette usually slips over the head. It provides an extra layer of protection between your boobs and the elements, as well as a minimal amount of support. As an added bonus, bralettes are usually sized small, medium, and large, so there's no need to calculate anything!

WHO IT'S FOR: The perfect starter bra, or for girls with smaller breasts who don't need a lot of support yet want an extra layer of fabric between their nipples and their clothing.

TRIANGLE

WHAT IT DOES: This soft-cup (meaning wireless) bra has minimal support and is similar to a bralette, yet it comes in regular bra sizes and with a clasp in back.

WHO IT'S FOR: Most comfortable for girls with small boobs.

SPORTS

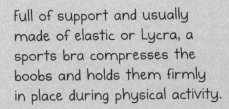

WHAT IT DOES: Full of support and usually made of elastic or Lycra, a sports bra compresses the boobs and holds them firmly in place during physical activity.

WHO IT'S FOR: Good for basketball stars, soccer stars, and running-for-the-school-bus stars.

	WHAT IT DOES	**WHO IT'S FOR**

UNDERWIRE

You guessed it: This one has wires underneath the cups. Underwire bras lift the boobs and hold them in place.

Great for girls with medium to large boobs who are looking for a little more support.

FULL-FIGURE

Like a backpack (or front pack) for your boobs, with thick and sometimes cushioned straps, a wide back, extra hooks, and complete breast coverage, a full-figure bra gives the maximum amount of support. It's especially good if the weight of your boobs is physically painful.

Only for girls with large boobs. In fact, most full-figure bras don't even come in A and B sizes.

NO BRA!

As magical as skinny-dipping in Lake Silver Moon on a warm summer night, wearing no bra sets your boobies freeeeeeeee.

Anyone! If your breasts don't hurt or feel like they've gone off course when you go braless, then the No Bra can be for you. Substitute a tank top or camisole if you want an extra layer of warmth while still feeling free.

Bras come in all sorts of fun fabrics, colors, and patterns, from blue cotton polka dots to orange lace. But while you may be tempted to buy every bra in the store, wait until your boobs stop growing before you splurge. I'm STILL thinking about that neon-green bra I outgrew after only one wear! —GRACE

If you find that perfect bra—affordable, comfortable, cute, fits perfectly, and gives you just the right amount of support—buy two, or even three, because it will almost definitely be discontinued exactly one month before your first one falls apart.

—Makayla

ABBY'S TIP FOR LATE BLOOMERS

Flat-as-a-pancake till sixteen? Sharing underwear is a big no-no, but sharing bras is A-OK! If your boobs are developing a little (or a lot) later than your friends' boobs are, use it to your advantage and double your wardrobe by calling dibs on that pink striped bra your best friend is about to bust out of.

Grace, will you be my BREAST friend?

That depends. What do I have to do?

Well, you would go bra shopping with me.

I love bra shopping!

And you would give me the bras you've outgrown.

No problem!

OK, but don't forget that neon-green one...

Over my dead body!

THE BOOBIE BATTLE BOOK: OR, HOW TO PUT ON A BRA

OK, you bought a bra. **Now you have to put it on.** (Eek!) There are two ways to put on a back-clasping bra. Followers of each bra-donning camp will swear up and down that their way is the right way, but we promise both are equally correct, even if it sometimes feels like act two of The Butter Battle Book, but with bras.

METHOD 1: THE CLASP-BEHIND, AS DEMONSTRATED BY Jenna

1. Put your arms through your bra straps as if you're putting on a button-down shirt backward.

2. Reach behind you and grab both ends of the unhooked band.

3. Clasp the hooks together, and voilà!

METHOD 2: THE CLASP-IN-FRONT, AS DEMONSTRATED BY EMMA L.

1. Wrap the band around your midsection so that the clasp is against your stomach, facing out. (Leave your arms out of it this time.) You'll want to make sure you're not putting the bra on upside down.

2. Hook the bra, then shimmy it around your waist so the cups are now in front.

3. Thread your arms through the straps, and voilà!

Both methods may require some final adjusting. You'll want the band to sit underneath your boobs and the straps to fit snugly but not tightly. If you find that your bra straps fall off your shoulders throughout the day, they need to be tightened. If you come home and see indentation marks against your skin, by all means LOOSEN UP!

Or do what I do and avoid the boobie battle altogether by wearing a front-clasping bra! —Makayla

PROPER KEEPING OF BRAS
for Proper (and Improper) Ladies

Let's get one thing out of the way here: **You do NOT need to wash your bra after every wear.** Not even after every two wears. After three, give it the sniff test and decide if you can get one more day out of it. But you max out at four wears before you are officially gross. (This does not apply to sports bras. If you do some heavy sweating, toss that bra in the wash.)

When it IS finally time to wash your bra, here are some tips to get it right:

1. Whenever possible, **WASH YOUR BRAS BY HAND.** Bras are delicate, and they only work when they hold their shape.

2. If washing your bras by hand is too much of a hassle (most of us have never once hand-washed our bras, so we get it), consider buying a mesh bag that's meant to protect your delicates. Stick all your bras inside, zip it up, and toss it in the washing machine with the rest of your clothes. This is especially important for underwire bras, which have been known to lose their underwires in washing machines.

> Washing machines are NOTORIOUS for stretching out bras. A few minutes of hand-washing could mean adding years of life to your bra.
> —Makayla

3. Always, always air-dry. Lay your bras flat to dry (so gravity doesn't mess with their shape). You'll thank us later.

NOW FOR THAT OTHER KIND OF TISSUE...

THE TOP FIVE REASONS TO JUST SAY NO TO STUFFING YOUR BRA
(AS LEARNED THE HARD WAY BY GRACE):

#1
Your boobs will appear **LUMPY**.

#2
You might lose a tissue...

#3
...or <u>SIX</u>.

#4
Then you'll forever be known as "McTissue"...

#5
...when you could just be known as (YOUR NAME).

PUT YOUR BEST BREAST FORWARD:
ONE LAST WORD ON BOOBS AND BRAS

It's perfectly natural to look around and wonder, "What would my boobs look like if they were a different size?" After all, with so many shapes and sizes out there, it's almost impossible not to be curious. But the truth is, YOUR breasts are the best breasts.

If you don't believe us, here is a handy guide to the top reasons to love your boobs in the size they are.

WHY TO LOVE YOUR SMALL BOOBS:

You can easily skip wearing a bra any day of the week. Wearing a strapless dress and don't have a strapless bra? Go braless! Forgot to do laundry? Go braless! Want to feel the wind against your skin? Go braless! But it's not just about how easy it is to set your boobs free. You also have the benefit of sleeping on your stomach, running, or doing jumping jacks with minimal discomfort.

—Abby, SAGE, and Jenna

WHY TO LOVE YOUR IN-BETWEEN BOOBS:

Clothes were made for you! You don't have to worry about dresses or button-down shirts being too loose or too tight. And you can buy bra and underwear sets without having to mix and match sizes. You have the Goldilocks of boobs. Enjoy them!

—EMMA L., Emma R., GRACE, and Lea

WHY TO LOVE YOUR BIG BOOBS:

We have one word for you: CLEAVAGE! There's no question about it—big boobs can make a statement. And while you don't always have to make that statement, it is nice to have the option. Plus your cleavage makes an excellent storage bin in case you don't feel like carrying your sunscreen down to the lake in your hand. And speaking of lakes...boobs float! True, they won't keep you from drowning, but next time you're swimming in Lake Silver Moon, watch how cool they look bobbing on the surface. Just don't forget to tread water!

—Brianna and Makayla

Camp Silver Moon
WEEK 4

IN WHICH EMMA L. GETS HER PERIOD AND, WITH A LITTLE HELP FROM HER FRIENDS, **CELEBRATES WOMANHOOD WITH A BIG SPLASH.**

On the morning of July 26,
EMMA L. GOT HER PERIOD.
She wasn't the first of us to get her period (that honor went to Emma R.). She wasn't even the first of us to get her period that summer—Makayla and Emma R. had both gotten theirs earlier in July, and Brianna complained nonstop that hers was about to come. But Emma L. was **the first—and ONLY—one of us to get <u>HER VERY FIRST PERIOD</u> at Camp Silver Moon.**

Emma L.'s discovery came right before Morning Swim. It wasn't even 10 a.m., and the temperature outside was already pushing 90 degrees, which meant she was not, under any circumstances, going to miss Morning Swim. Unfortunately, Emma L. could not seem to unlock the ins and outs (but especially the ins) of *using a tampon*. In other words, SHE COULDN'T GET THE TAMPON IN. And then she did get it in, but only halfway. The rest of us weren't much help. Makayla and Brianna both used pads at the time. So did our counselor Julia. Our other counselor, Collette, used tampons, but she was on her day off. Which left only Emma R. to help.

Like any true member of the Sisterhood, Emma R. was a terrific coach. She stood on the other side of the bathroom door and talked Emma L. through every step. She even gave her a tiny mirror in case a visual aid would help.

AND IT WORKED! OK, true, both the Emmas missed Morning Swim. But when Afternoon Swim came around, they jumped into the lake side by side. And we all committed Emma R.'s tips to memory, in case we needed to use them later.

Because every first period deserves a period party, we threw one right after dinner. We made Emma L. a crown out of panty liners (clean ones!) and had goody bags filled with chocolate. We played womanly songs and danced around Emma L. like she was a maypole. And while it's the only one we got to attend, we think it's safe to say

IT'S THE BEST PERIOD PARTY
CAMP SILVER MOON HAS EVER SEEN.

It might not be Visiting Day at Camp Silver Moon, but Aunt Flo just pulled into the parking lot. UNINVITED. That's right, we're talking about the CRIMSON WAVE. THE RAG. SHARK WEEK. THAT TIME OF THE MONTH. Or, as Jenna likes to say, "LEAVE ME ALONE. MY LADY STORM IS HERE."

Women of Bunk 9, we have finally, officially, celebratoriously reached... THE PERIOD CHAPTER!!!!!

Yes, we made up the word CELEBRATORIOUSLY, and no, we're not going to cross it out. —EMMA L.

MENSTRUATION (THE BASICS)

Scientifically speaking, MENSTRUATION (that's men-stroo-AY-shun), or your **PERIOD**, is your body's way of telling you you're not pregnant. Not scientifically speaking, it's a usually monthly occurrence when you **BLEED out of your vagina**. WHAT?!! Yes. And also, yes, we know this sounds terrifying. But we promise there's nothing scary about it, even if it might take a little getting used to.

MENSTRUATION (THE INS AND OUTS)

Like most of the changes that happen during puberty, menstruation is a signal that your body is capable of having a baby. Once you start getting your period, your body prepares each month for the possibility of getting pregnant. When that doesn't happen (because, hello, not ready!), your body gives up and then starts over. Confused? We'll back up.

Remember when we talked about the reproductive system? We don't either, because it was way back in WEEK 1, and Very Important Topics such as boobs and acne have been discussed since then. So as a reminder, your reproductive system is made up of a bunch of parts—your **ovaries, fallopian tubes, uterus, cervix, and vagina**—that have just been hanging around since you were born. But when you go through puberty, everything *kicks into gear*.

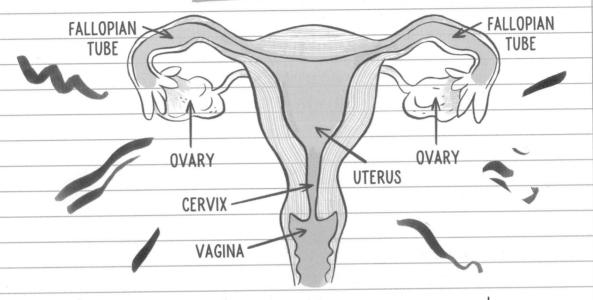

FALLOPIAN TUBE

FALLOPIAN TUBE

OVARY

OVARY

UTERUS

CERVIX

VAGINA

Once a month, your hormones cause your ovaries to release an egg. That egg travels through the fallopian tube to the uterus. This takes a few days, and while that's happening, the uterus gets all excited because it hears it's going to have company. The uterus starts building up a lining of blood and tissue to create a home for the egg in case it gets fertilized on its way and decides to stay and become a baby. Most months, fertilization doesn't happen, though. The uterus throws a big tantrum and kicks the egg out, tossing all of the interior decorations to the curb as well. Your cervix, which is like a tiny door, opens up slightly, and the egg, lining, and tissue flow through the vagina and out. *And hello, period!*

FERTILIZATION?

When the sperm from a male meets your egg, the egg can become FERTILIZED. But that happens only when a male and female have sexual intercourse without using birth control. In other words, YOU have control over whether fertilization happens.

You've probably heard not to put all of your eggs in one basket. Your body has heard that too, which is why you have two ovaries, but you release only one egg a month (except in the rare case of fraternal twins). While they don't take strict turns, they do divide the work. —Lea

Wait, before we go any further, can we take a quick detour? We keep talking about the reproductive system, but I think we're missing a very important piece of the puzzle: **THE VAGINA**. —SAGE

OMG, you're totally right! How could we skip the vagina?! —Makayla

OK, but technically, we're talking about THE VULVA. —EMMA L.

Vagina! Vagina! Vagina! Vagina! VAGINA! —Brianna

THE VAGINA (TECHNICALLY, THE VULVA)

You already know about your reproductive system on the inside, but what's happening on the outside? MAGIC.

Just kidding—it's your VULVA. But it IS kind of magical. In fact, if you've never taken a close look between your legs, grab a small handheld mirror and check things out. You can do this sitting on

your bed, lying on your back, or standing with one foot up on a chair or the toilet seat.

While you may know it as the *vagina*, the vagina is just a small part of the area you're looking at. The entire external area is actually called the VULVA (that's <u>VULL</u>-vah). It's your external reproductive system, or the female sex organs. Its job is to protect the internal reproductive system, and as a bonus it feels good to the touch!

But what are all of those parts and WHAT DO THEY DO?

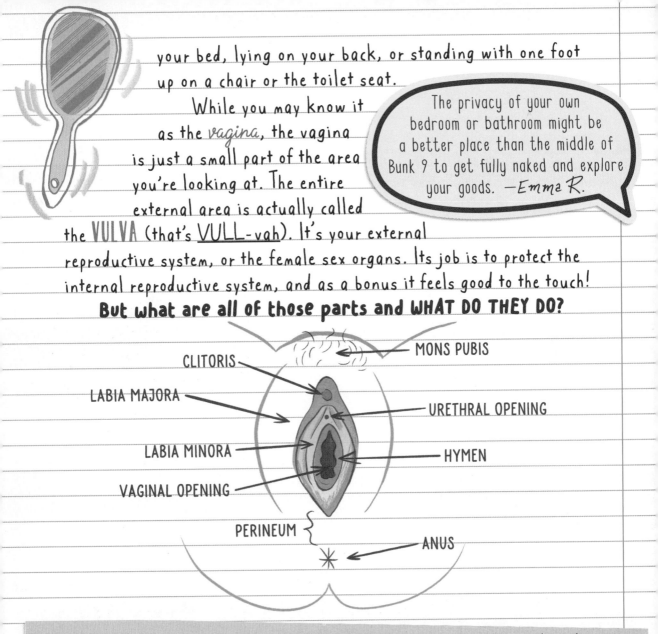

CLITORIS

LABIA MAJORA

LABIA MINORA

VAGINAL OPENING

MONS PUBIS

URETHRAL OPENING

HYMEN

PERINEUM

ANUS

<u>MONS PUBIS</u>: Literally, "pubic mountain." This is where you'll see most of your pubic hair.

<u>LABIA MAJORA</u>: Also known as the outer labia or outer lips, they cover and protect the other parts of the vulva. You'll see hair here as well.

<u>LABIA MINORA</u>: The inner labia or inner lips, these are the small, delicate folds of skin just inside the labia majora. They protect the vagina and add lubrication.

<u>CLITORIS</u>: The clitoris is the small hooded button at the top of your labia minora. It is completely packed with nerve endings, which makes it very sensitive to the touch. Its only job? To provide pleasure.

HYMEN: This is a piece of tissue that covers part of the vaginal opening. It can be thick or thin; it can have a small or large hole or sometimes even two holes; it can be very noticeable or barely there. With time it will probably be stretched or torn, something that can happen from riding a horse or bicycle, from inserting a tampon or your finger into your vagina, or from having sexual intercourse. Some women may bleed a little when their hymen is torn. For others, the hymen is so small to begin with that they don't notice the tear. And for others, the hole in the hymen is stretched over time but never actually tears.

VAGINAL OPENING: The entryway to your vagina. You can see only the opening, but inside is the vaginal canal, then the cervix, and then the uterus. The opening protects all of the interior parts. If you use tampons during your period, you insert them here.

URETHRAL OPENING: The small, top hole where your pee comes out.

TWO MORE FOR GOOD LUCK: Although they're not part of the vulva, you'll also see the perineum and anus. The **ANUS** is the opening in your butt, and the **PERINEUM** is the area between the bottom of your vulva and your anus.

Masturbation

Masturbation (that's mas-ter-BAY-shun) is the touching of one's own sex organs (for females, that's the vulva) for the purpose of pleasure. Masturbation is PERFECTLY NATURAL—after all, the clitoris's sole function is to provide pleasure—and most people enjoy getting to know their own body. You might find that you want to touch yourself a lot, you might not be interested in touching yourself at all, and you might fall somewhere in between. Remember that whether you masturbate or not is entirely your own choice. But do keep in mind that masturbation is a private act and should be done at home in your bedroom or bathroom and not in the middle of Bunk 9!

Did you know... the clitoris is the only organ in the female body whose entire job is to make you feel good? —SAGE

GET DISCHARGED!

What is **DISCHARGE?** It's a fluid that's secreted by your vagina to help flush out bacteria. (It's part of what makes your vagina self-cleaning.) It can be clear or milky, watery or thick like egg whites, and its color, texture, and amount often change throughout the month. You'll usually notice it a few months before you start your first period. You don't need to do anything about it—**IT WON'T LEAK** through your clothes, and it will wash out of your underwear when you do laundry—but if it leaves you feeling a bit wet or uncomfortable, **YOU CAN WEAR A PANTY LINER** (that's like a mini-pad), which will keep you dry and protect your underwear.

SOMETHING WONKY...

Usually your vagina doesn't need any special care, but occasionally, as with every part of your body, something goes a bit wonky. Here's what you should look for and when to consult a doctor:

YEAST INFECTIONS: Normal discharge can be clear or milky, thick or thin, but it *shouldn't be chunky* like cottage cheese. If it is (and it is accompanied by an itchy feeling), you might have a yeast infection. Try eating yogurt with probiotics—healthy bacteria—to see if it clears up on its own. Otherwise, talk to the nurse or a trusted adult. You may need a **PRESCRIPTION MED.** Wearing a wet bathing suit for too long can sometimes cause yeast infections, so always change right after Swim.

BACTERIAL INFECTIONS: It's normal to have slightly yellow discharge, which might even look a bit green when dried on undies, but a **DEEP YELLOW** or **GREEN DISCHARGE** combined with a nasty smell or discomfort could be a sign of a bacterial infection. Best to head over to the camp infirmary.

URINARY TRACT INFECTIONS: A UTI or bladder infection occurs when bacteria find their way into your urethra. It can cause a *painful sensation when you pee* and make you feel like you need to pee urgently and ALL the time. You'll want to check into the infirmary for fast relief (aka an antibiotic). Help avoid a UTI by always wiping from front to back.

105

THE PERIOD!

EMMA L.'S GUIDE TO ROCKING YOUR FIRST PERIOD

The summer we were twelve, I got my first period, but it didn't catch me ENTIRELY unprepared. That's because before you get your first period, you'll have gone through many of the other stages of puberty.

So how can you tell when your period is going to start and avoid wearing a pad when you don't have to?

1. You'll see the **FIRST SIGNS OF BREAST GROWTH** (those breast buds we discussed) about two years before you start your period. So if nothing has happened up top, you probably don't have to worry about anything happening down below. True, only one of my boobs was growing, but the one I had was really, really there!

> Meanwhile, that summer I was SO worried I was about to get my period that I wore a pad EVERY. SINGLE. DAY. Never mind that I had barely started going through puberty and didn't get my period for another two years after that. If I had only known!
>
> —Jenna

106

2. You'll have **PUBIC HAIR**. You'll usually see it about a year before you get your period. If you haven't seen at least a little growth, you've got some time before your period comes.

3. You'll see white stuff in your underwear. A few months or more before your period starts, you'll begin having discharge—a clear or milky fluid that's secreted by your vagina. Once you start getting discharge, it's probably a good idea to have a couple of pads handy.

4. In the week before you get your period, you might notice that your breasts feel a bit sore and that you're more cranky than usual, and you may even have some cramping in the area a few inches below your belly button. Those are some of the signs of premenstrual syndrome, or PMS (more on that later), and you might feel them every month before your period. Guess what... it's almost here!

> If you're experiencing sore breasts and abdominal cramps, chances are your **PERIOD IS COMING ANY DAY** now. Consider wearing a panty liner to help protect your underwear, and make sure you have a couple of pads on hand. —GRACE

5. When your first period finally does arrive, **switch that panty liner out for a regular pad**—you'll need it! Clean yourself the same way you would wipe when you pee or poop. Then find your best friend, counselor, camp nurse, teacher, or parent and let them know. They'll be able to walk you through what's next, and congratulate you, of course!

CYCLE BACK

The term **MENSTRUAL CYCLE** refers to everything that happens to your reproductive system from **the first day of your period until it starts again**. A typical menstrual cycle is twenty-eight to thirty-five days, but it can be as short as twenty-one days or as long as forty-five.

Day one of your cycle is the day you start your period. Ovulation (or the release of the egg from the ovary) happens about two weeks later, depending on the length of your cycle. The last day of your cycle is the day before you get your next period. Why count the days? Knowing how long your cycle is can help you figure out when you'll get your next period. Some women have cycles that are exactly the same number of days each month, while other women have cycles that fluctuate a little or a lot. Make a habit of **marking your calendar or journal on the FIRST DAY OF YOUR PERIOD**, to get a sense of your own cycle. After all, if you know your cycle is usually anywhere from twenty-nine to thirty-one days, you'll know when to shove a pad in your pocket just in case.

The first time I got my period, I was eleven, but I didn't get it again for almost an entire year. Many girls have irregular cycles in the beginning. They may get their period every three months during the first year, or they may get it once and then not get it again for six months. Things usually become more regular within a year or two. —Brianna

On the flip side, after I got mine that summer it came like clockwork on the twenty-sixth of every single month, whether the month had thirty, thirty-one, or twenty-eight days—leap years too! —EMMA L.

EVERYTHING. (PERIOD)

IN WHICH WE TELL YOU <u>EXACTLY</u> WHAT TO EXPECT.

GIVE IT TO ME IN DAYS.

Most women's periods last between _three and five days_, but your period can be as short as two days or as long as seven.

> I totally thought it would be blood like when you scrape your knee. So when it was dark and kind of thick, I thought I was dying. OBVIOUSLY.
> —Lea

AND THE BLOOD?

Your period is a mix of blood, tissue, and lining from your uterus, so it won't look like the blood from a cut. Instead, expect something **THICKER**, especially in the first day or two, when it **MIGHT EVEN HAVE CLUMPS** in it (these are small blood clots and they are totally NORMAL). It can range in color from **BRIGHT RED** to **DARK BROWN**, but it's usually redder at first and brown toward the end of your period.

JUST HOW MUCH BLOOD ARE WE TALKING ABOUT?

That varies. Although it might seem like gallons, typically you'll see about **TWO to THREE tablespoons of MENSTRUAL FLUID** during your period (that includes everything, not just blood, which is why it's called fluid). But if your period is light, it can be as little as one tablespoon, and if it's heavy, as much as six tablespoons. Everyone's period is different!

> Not only is everyone's period different, but your own period can be different from month to month. I have months where my period is heavy, and others when it's really light! —GRACE

DOES IT ALL COME GUSHING OUT?

Thankfully, **NO**. Most women will have just a trickle at first, giving you enough time to grab a pad or tampon and run to the bathroom. The **FIRST TWO OR THREE DAYS ARE THE HEAVIEST**, and after that your period will taper off, with each day becoming a bit lighter. By the last day of your period, you might see only a tiny bit of blood.

WILL IT HURT?

Maybe. Your uterus contracts to shed the lining it built up. When it does, you might feel cramps in the area about two or three inches below your belly button. They can start a couple of days before your period and usually last through the first or second day. Cramps are

sometimes accompanied by lower-back pain, and you might also feel a dull pain in your cervix as it opens up to let the menstrual fluid pass through. Some women experience a lot of cramping, others none at all, and for some it changes from month to month. But if you're in severe pain each month, talk to your doctor to make sure everything is OK.

My cramps leave me wanting to curl up in the fetal position, but luckily they only last a day. My period, on the other hand, takes its sweet time for seven days. —Makayla

I have months when I barely notice my cramps at all, and others when my cramps are so bad I think I'm going to throw up from the pain. You can guess which months I like more! —Lea

ANYTHING ELSE?

As if five days of bleeding weren't enough, your period can also AFFECT YOUR POOP. If you notice that you have to poop a lot more (or less) during your period, and you suddenly experience diarrhea or constipation, it is, unfortunately, normal.

I basically don't leave the bathroom on the first day of my period, thanks to period poop. —Brianna

Ewwww, Brianna, no one wants to know about your poop! —Jenna

What?! It's a totally legitimate comment. I have nonstop diarrhea during my period. The Sisterhood needs to know! —Brianna

THE BUNK 9 SURVIVAL MANUAL

While there are definitely good things about your period (You've become a woman! Your body is telling you it's operating normally!), we're not going to pretend like your period needs to be celebrated every. single. month. Most months, it just needs to be survived. And like any proper survivor, you need gear. Good gear.

PADS, TAMPONS, PERIOD UNDERWEAR. When it comes to catching menstrual fluids, there's no shortage of options. Use our guide to help you pick what's right for you. And there's no rule that says you can't mix and match.

PADS → WHAT THEY ARE

If you've heard the term "on the rag," it originates from the rags women once placed in their underwear during their periods. Luckily, those rags have since been upgraded to pads. Disposable, absorbent, and sticky on one side, the pad goes in your underwear and collects menstrual fluids.

HOW TO USE ONE

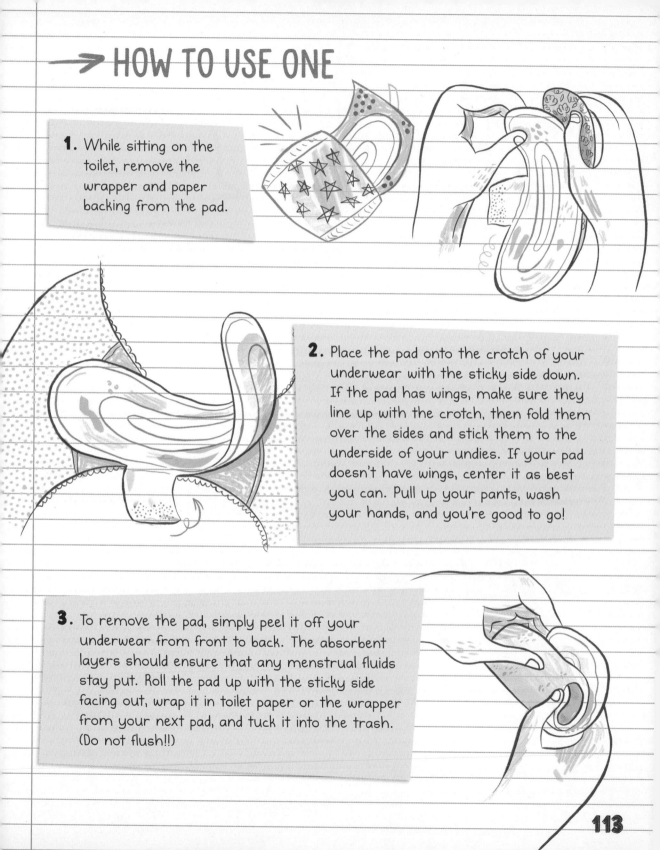

1. While sitting on the toilet, remove the wrapper and paper backing from the pad.

2. Place the pad onto the crotch of your underwear with the sticky side down. If the pad has wings, make sure they line up with the crotch, then fold them over the sides and stick them to the underside of your undies. If your pad doesn't have wings, center it as best you can. Pull up your pants, wash your hands, and you're good to go!

3. To remove the pad, simply peel it off your underwear from front to back. The absorbent layers should ensure that any menstrual fluids stay put. Roll the pad up with the sticky side facing out, wrap it in toilet paper or the wrapper from your next pad, and tuck it into the trash. (Do not flush!!)

→ THE LOWDOWN

HOW OFTEN TO CHANGE	Every 3 to 4 hours, depending on your flow. Even with a light flow, you'll want to change your pad to prevent odor and bacteria.
SWIMMING	No, no, no!!
SPORTS	Yes, but proceed with caution.
SLEEP	Absolutely! Choose an extra-long pad and sleep soundly.
EASE OF USE	Yes, yes, yes!! It's hard to mess up pads.
PROS	They're easy to use.
CONS	They're not eco-friendly, they can sometimes feel a bit bulky, and forget the lake!

> If you're playing sports, use a pad with wings and pair it with well-fitting panties to prevent the pad from moving around. —GRACE

> Winging it? Wings are small flaps on your pad that tuck around the sides and bottom of your underwear to help prevent leakage. However, some women find that they can't position the pad exactly how they want to with wings, so consider them optional! —Brianna

TAMPONS → WHAT THEY ARE

Kind of like a plug, a tampon is inserted into the vagina to absorb menstrual fluids before they have a chance to reach your underwear. It often has an applicator for easy insertion, and has a string for easy removal.

→ HOW TO USE ONE

1. With clean hands, remove the tampon from the wrapper. If you're using a compact tampon, gently pull apart the two parts of the applicator to extend it to its full length. You should feel or hear it click into place.

2. Stand with your legs apart and slightly bent, like you're about to sit down on a chair, or half squat.

The string goes at the bottom!

3. Holding the applicator where its two parts meet, gently guide the tampon into your vagina until the entire top section of the applicator is inside. Press the plunger part of the applicator until it stops. (If it hurts going in, stop, pull the tampon out, and talk to a parent or another trusted adult. Lubricant may also help.)

4. With the tampon securely inside, pull on the applicator to remove both parts. Wrap it in a tampon wrapper and toss it in the trash. You're ready to face the world—just don't forget to wash your hands!

more on next page!

5. To remove the tampon, gently pull the string down and away from you. If it's slippery, try wrapping the string around one finger. Wrap the tampon in toilet paper and throw it away. Do not flush. Do not flush! DO NOT FLUSH!!!

Seriously, do not flush. Unless, of course, you want to have to call George the maintenance guy and have him lecture you about clogging the septic system. —*Emma R.*

→ THE LOWDOWN

HOW OFTEN TO CHANGE	You can safely wear a tampon for up to eight hours. However, you'll have to change it more often on heavy-flow days. Tampons have different absorbencies, and you should always use the smallest tampon possible. So, while you might use a regular or super tampon on the first two days of your period, you should use a light tampon toward the end. Luckily, most tampon brands sell multipacks with a variety of absorbencies.
SWIMMING	Splash away!!
SPORTS	Yes! And exercise can help with cramps.
SLEEP	We're always optimistic that we'll get more than eight hours of sleep. Plus it doesn't hurt to let your vagina breathe a bit overnight. We usually choose a pad or period panties for overnight wear, and reserve tampons for daytime use.

Always, always check that you removed your old tampon before putting in a new one. —*Jenna*

Do a string check before swimming with a tampon to make sure the string of your tampon isn't sticking out of your bathing suit. —*Makayla*

EASE OF USE	It can take some time to figure out how to insert them—but once you get the hang of it, it's as easy as 1-2-3-4-5.
PROS	Swimming, sports, no problem!
CONS	Until you figure out how to get them in (and out!), they're an impenetrable mystery!

While most tampons have applicators, every once in a while you might come across one that doesn't (like if you borrow a tampon from Sage). To insert a tampon that doesn't have an applicator, first pull on the string to widen the base and create a pocket for your finger. Holding the tampon at the base, guide it into your vagina. Then continue to insert it using your middle or index finger. The pocket you created will keep your fingertip clean. Remove it like you would any other tampon. —EMMA L.

Non-applicator tampons aren't just a last resort! They're easy to insert and much, much better for the environment. —SAGE

For a while I was scared to try tampons because I was worried one would get sucked into my uterus and disappear there. You'll be relieved to know that definitely isn't going to happen. Even though your cervix opens up a bit during your period, there is no way it will open up enough to let a tampon pass through. Promise. —Lea

If you're the forgetful type, set an alarm to remind you to change your tampon. Just, you know, don't forget to set that alarm. —Abby

TTYL, TSS.

While tampons are generally very safe, there's a small risk of getting **TOXIC SHOCK SYNDROME (TSS)**, a dangerous bacterial infection, from tampon use. To avoid TSS, NEVER leave a tampon in for longer than eight hours, and always use the smallest size your flow will allow. You should also never use a tampon when you DON'T have your period. If you think you might be getting your period and want to play it safe, use a pad, panty liner, or period underwear (see the next page) to avoid any surprises.

PERIOD UNDERWEAR

→ WHAT THEY ARE

Underwear that you wear during your period! These special underpants look like their regular sisters, but they're made of an absorbent material that holds in menstrual fluids.

→ HOW TO USE THEM

1. Put on underwear. Go!
2. Every brand is different—so always read the instructions on the package—but you'll usually have to hand-rinse the panties before you throw them in the washing machine and hang to dry.

→ THE LOWDOWN

HOW OFTEN TO CHANGE	That depends on the brand. Some are made to replace tampons or pads; others are made to be used as backup. But even those that provide the most coverage max out at the equivalent of two tampons of menstrual fluid. Which means if you're wearing them solo, they might not be the best choice on your heaviest day.
SWIMMING	Maybe. Some brands look almost like bathing suits, and the whole point is that they're meant to hold liquids. We wouldn't test this out in a pool on your heaviest day, but in Lake Silver Moon, where the water is already murky, we've given it a go on a medium-flow day and no one has known.

SPORTS	Yes, please!
SLEEP	Definitely.
EASE OF USE	We could skip having to rinse them in the sink, but other than that they're as easy to use as non-period underwear.
PROS	They're reusable, which makes them earth-friendly. And they feel just like underwear.
CONS	They're risky on your heaviest days, and they're pricey (especially when you think you'll probably need a week's worth to make it through your entire period), so it's probably best to hold off on these until you've finished growing.

I have two pairs of period underwear. I wear them when I'm worried my period is coming but don't want to run to the bathroom every ten minutes to check. And I wear them on my medium and light days. And I wash them in between. —Jenna

A TALE OF TWO PERIOD PANTIES

(A) Old underwear that you should probably throw out already, but which are perfect for wearing during your period, because who cares if your pad overflows and stains them?

(B) Special underwear made of absorbent and waterproof materials that you can wear instead of a tampon or pad if your period is light, or as backup against leaks if your period is heavy.

We know you've been waiting for Emma R.'s tips for tampon use. We all committed them to memory, and we highly recommend you do too. —Abby

EMMA R.'S TIPS FOR

RELAX. Inserting a tampon will be nearly *impossible* if you're clenching your vagina.

CHANGE YOUR POSITION. While half squatting is usually the easiest, it's a difficult position to hold while also relaxing (see above). Try either sitting on the toilet as far back as possible and reaching between your legs or standing with one foot up on the toilet seat.

FEEL FOR AN OPENING. Finding the opening of your vagina can be a little tricky. Slide the tip of the tampon around to try and feel for it.

SAGE'S GUIDE TO A GREEN PERIOD

The average woman will have about 450 PERIODS in her life. When you multiply the number of pads and tampons you use each month by 450, that's a whole lot of trash. Here are a few ways you can go green while you're seeing red:

✽ Whenever possible, **use all-cotton pads and tampons.** Some brands even have biodegradable or compostable pads, which are made without plastic.

FIRST-TIME TAMPON USE

USE A VISUAL AID. If sliding the tampon around doesn't do the trick, TRY USING A HANDHELD MIRROR to find the opening of your vagina. (This will be easiest with one foot up on the toilet seat. Place the mirror on the closed toilet lid, or hold it in the same hand as the leg that's up, and hold the tampon with your other hand.)

CHECK YOUR ANGLE. The instinct is to insert in an upward direction, but the vagina is actually tilted, which means your tampon needs to be inserted at an angle. Try to aim the tampon toward the top of your butt/tailbone. If that doesn't work, aim lower and farther back, or a little to the left or to the right.

TRY AGAIN. Eventually you'll figure it out! (And if you don't, that's OK too—there are other options.)

☆ If you use pads, **switch to a panty liner for the last day or two of your period** (if your flow is light enough). They're smaller and therefore will create less trash.

☆ Consider using **applicator-free** tampons. While the tampon itself still creates trash, ditching the applicator is a definite step in the right direction.

☆ Look into reusable products, such as **washable pads, period underwear,** or, for advanced period goers, the **menstrual cup** (a small, washable cup that's inserted into the vagina to collect fluid).

SAY IT LOUD, SAY IT PROUD!

While we think all members of the Sisterhood should shout from the rooftops (or porches) when they get their period, we understand that it can be hard to talk about. Whether you're asking your dad to pick up pads or you're bringing a box of tampons up to the register at the store, here are a few tips on how to get through those (potentially) awkward moments.

Talk to your mom (or dad) before you get your first period, so you don't find yourself in an urgent situation. Ask them if they can buy you some supplies just in case. They'll probably be thrilled you're willing to talk to them! —Abby

Don't blink. Whether you're asking your mom what kind of tampon is the best kind or you're bringing those tampons up to the register, if you act like it's no big deal, then it won't be. —Makayla

Use email, text them, or leave them a note. I have two dads, and there was NO. WAY. I was asking them to buy pads for me. I sent them a link to the kind that Grace recommended, and they appeared on my bed the next day, along with a printout from a website explaining what my period is. I was SO relieved. —Jenna

Remember, every single woman who has gone through puberty has gotten her period. No matter who you're talking to, you won't be the first person they've encountered who has menstruated. —Emma R.

Practice. This is a good idea for any conversation you might find difficult to have. Grab a friend and ask them to practice with you. —SAGE

Enlist help. I really didn't want to ask my mom for pads, so I asked Emma L.'s mom to ask her for me. My mom then started the conversation with me, which was so much easier. —GRACE

GET PACKING!

You wouldn't show up to Camp Silver Moon without packing, and the same should go for your period. But while you don't need to carry around a duffel bag just because you're menstruating, you do need to carry something. After all, if you throw a loose tampon into your backpack before the camp trip to the amusement park, and add one tuna sandwich, a carton of milk, and a damp towel, you will end up with a completely unusable tampon and a moment of PANIC at the top of the roller coaster.

Which means a *Period Pouch* is definitely a good idea. Use it to store tampons, pads, panty liners, an extra pair of undies, and cramp remedies, so you're never unprepared. A small zippered pouch, cosmetics bag, or soft pencil case is the right size to transport your tampon from Arts & Crafts to the nearest bathroom. And if you're feeling bold, go ahead and use the BeDazzler in the Arts & Crafts shed to add the words **WOMAN, PERIOD, or LADY STORM** to your pouch—after all, **YOUR PERIOD IS A BADGE OF HONOR!**

> Not that we know this from experience or anything.
> —Makayla

> If you forget your Period Pouch, slip a pad or tampon into your pocket or up your sleeve to get it to the bathroom unnoticed. Or carry it out in the open, because why not?! —Brianna

> If you don't have anything handy, ask a friend. But on the rare occasions when the moon and stars line up to leave you without any protection, fold a large wad of toilet paper or paper towel into the shape of a pad and tuck it into your underwear. —Emma R.

STOP CRAMPING MY STYLE!

If you're going to survive your period, you're going to *need to survive cramps.* Whether your cramps are mild enough to mostly ignore or so severe you want to curl up in a ball, these remedies will help get you out of bed and to Music Under the Big Tree without Counselor Julia having to drag you out of your sleeping bag.

1. Exercise. No, this is not a trick. Exercise increases blood circulation, which helps alleviate cramps. Not only that, but it relieves stress, which also contributes to cramps. For the best results, try to get some aerobic exercise at least three times a week all month, whether it's running, swimming, soccer, or dance. And when the cramps hit hard, lace up your sneakers and go for a jog around Camp Silver Moon. —SAGE

2. Find your inner yogi. Gentle yoga stretches can help open up your abdominal area when it's feeling cramped. Try RESTORATIVE POSES like camel, cobra, seated forward bend, and child's pose for pain relief during that time of the month. —Emma R.

3. **Apply heat.** Lie down with a hot-water bottle, or stick an adhesive heating pad under your clothes to help relax your uterus. It will help with cramps AND with cold nights at Camp Silver Moon. Soaking in a hot bath—although impossible at camp—may also help. —Jenna

4. **Cozy up with a cup of tea.** Herbal teas such as CHAMOMILE, GINGER, and PEPPERMINT will warm you up from the inside and help relax you—two things that are good for cramps. —EMMA L.

5. **Take pain medication.** If your cramps are so bad that the natural remedies above don't do the trick, an over-the-counter painkiller, such as IBUPROFEN OR ACETAMINOPHEN, can help. Always check with your parent or guardian before taking any medication, and carefully read the label to ensure a proper dose. —Makayla

> Cramps are an unfortunate reality of having your period, but if you're experiencing so much pain that none of these remedies helps, you should talk to your doctor to make sure nothing more serious is going on. —Brianna

PERIOD HYGIENE

Good news! Personal hygiene while you have your period looks a lot like personal hygiene during the rest of the month. Shower daily when you're on your period and use your hand or a washcloth along with warm water and a mild, unscented soap to gently clean the area around your labia and vaginal opening.

PMS

HEY!! —Brianna

Are you feeling a bit more emotional than usual? Do you wish Brianna would just stop talking? Do you think you might cry because nothing came for you in today's mail? Are your boobs sore? Do you want to raid the Bunk 9 candy trunk? Did you wake up with a giant zit? If you said yes, yes, and yes, welcome to PMS. (That's PreMenstrual Syndrome, and it refers to a range of changes that may occur shortly before your period comes each month.)

   If none of the above sounds fun, we totally understand. But while some of it is unavoidable—sadly, premenstrual pimples are part of the territory for many of us—there are a few things you can do to help combat PMS. Exercise regularly to keep your mood stable all month, take a momentary "time-out" and breathe deeply if you feel like you're on the edge, and resist those food cravings whenever possible, as a sugar high now will leave you crashing later. Trust us—we know.

The moods and emotions that come with PMS can last into the first couple of days of your period. I cry on the second day of my period almost every month. About stupid things—like running out of cornflakes, or not being able to find my favorite pair of shoes. —Lea

THERE'S A SPILL IN AISLE 6...

With an average of 450 periods in your lifetime, the odds are good that eventually you'll have an accident. But whether you leak through your favorite skirt or wake up to discover blood on your mattress, **DON'T PANIC.** Once you're done not-panicking, do the following:

UNDERWEAR, CLOTHES, AND SHEETS:

Rinse the stain in cold water with a little soap or laundry detergent, and then toss the item into a cold-water wash. Repeat as necessary. If the underwear stain doesn't come out on its own, you can now consider this a pair of period panties (A) (as in old underwear you wear during your period).

MATTRESSES:

Dab the stain with a damp paper towel (cold water only!). Then use an oxygen-based laundry spray on the area and let it sit for a day. If that doesn't work, try making a paste of water and either salt or baking soda, and use a Q-tip to apply it to the area. Let it sit for a few hours, then remove the paste with a damp paper towel. You don't want to soak the mattress, however, so whether you're applying laundry spray or a salt paste, do so lightly. And remember, a stained mattress is just part of being a woman!

MENSTRUATION CELEBRATION
(OR, ONE LAST THING ABOUT PERIODS)

Members of the Silver Moon Sisterhood: If you've been following this chapter closely, you might be thinking that having your period sounds like a huge pain in the BUTT. You're wrong—it's a **huge pain in the UTERUS**.

BUT! It's also something to be celebrated. Because it means you are a woman! It doesn't matter if you get your first period at age nine, like Emma R., or at sixteen, like Abby; every first period deserves to be CELEBRATED. And as a member of the Sisterhood, it's your job to help your fellow sisters do the celebrating. Whether you BeDazzle a Period Pouch for your BFF, like Grace did for Jenna, or throw a period party, like we all did for Emma L., here are a few ideas to get you started:

Make a Period Crown

WHAT YOU NEED

construction paper

scissors

stapler

glue

glitter or markers

7 to 10 panty liners (the kind that do NOT come pre-folded)

Use regular panty liners for a tall crown. To create a spiked crown apply panty liners made for thong underwear, with the wide part at the bottom. —Jenna

WHAT TO DO

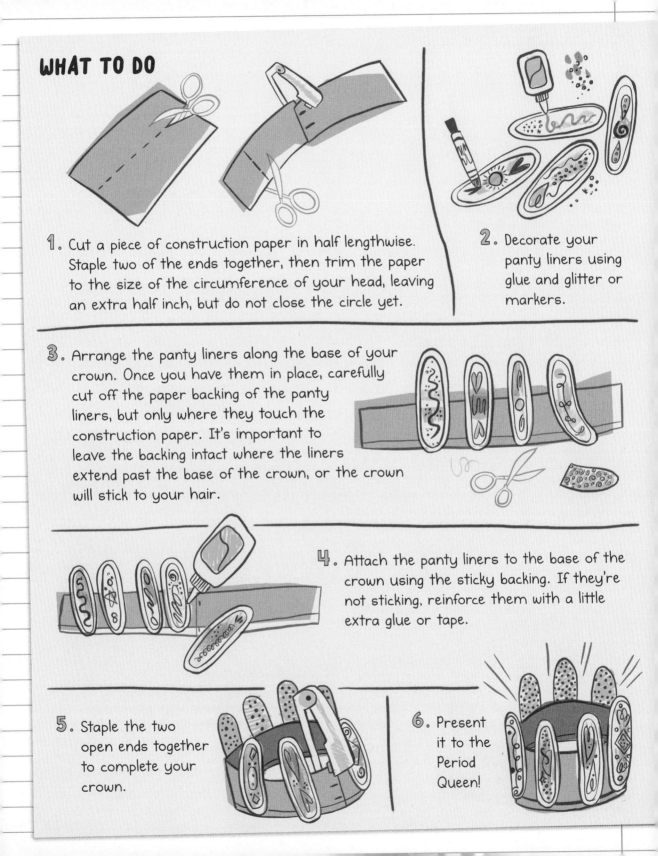

1. Cut a piece of construction paper in half lengthwise. Staple two of the ends together, then trim the paper to the size of the circumference of your head, leaving an extra half inch, but do not close the circle yet.

2. Decorate your panty liners using glue and glitter or markers.

3. Arrange the panty liners along the base of your crown. Once you have them in place, carefully cut off the paper backing of the panty liners, but only where they touch the construction paper. It's important to leave the backing intact where the liners extend past the base of the crown, or the crown will stick to your hair.

4. Attach the panty liners to the base of the crown using the sticky backing. If they're not sticking, reinforce them with a little extra glue or tape.

5. Staple the two open ends together to complete your crown.

6. Present it to the Period Queen!

Make a Period Mixtape

Give your BFF a playlist of songs about being a woman. A few suggestions:

* ☆ "Girl on Fire" by Alicia Keys
* ☆ "Brave" by Sara Bareilles
* ☆ "I'm Not a Girl, Not Yet a Woman" by Britney Spears
* ☆ "I Am Woman" by Helen Reddy
* ☆ "Girls Just Want to Have Fun" by Cyndi Lauper
* ☆ "Shake It Off" by Taylor Swift
* ☆ "I'm Every Woman" by Chaka Khan
* ☆ "Edge of Seventeen" by Stevie Nicks
* ☆ "Roar" by Katy Perry
* ☆ "You Don't Own Me" by Lesley Gore

* ☆ "The Greatest" by Sia
* ☆ "Sisters Are Doin' It for Themselves" by Eurythmics and Aretha Franklin

Give Her a Chocolate Bar

OK, OK. We know we said you should avoid giving in to those chocolate cravings. But we think you can make an exception if it's a FIRST period. Nothing says Menstruation Celebration like a candy bar with a bow on top. Just make sure you get your BFF the one SHE likes rather than the one you like.

Camp Silver Moon

WEEK 5

IN WHICH MAKAYLA DISCOVERS A FEW SECRETS ABOUT BUNK 8, AND EVERYONE ELSE **GAINS BOTH VALUABLE AND UNWANTED KNOWLEDGE.**

Nate was the fastest boy in Bunk 8, and the second fastest kid in the Twelves (only Sage was faster). He was also THE NICEST and knew how to make friendship bracelets with eighteen strings. It's fair to say that half of Bunk 9 had a crush on him.

Unfortunately for the rest of us, Nate had a crush on only one girl in Bunk 9: **MAKAYLA**. He asked her to go out with him midway through summer, and she immediately said YES. Going out meant they held hands on the way to dinner and sat next to each other during evening activities like Camp-Wide Movie Night. But for everyone else, Makayla and Nate going out meant only one thing: WE had access to the BOYS. Well, Makayla did. And sometimes Brianna and Abby did too.

It's not that we weren't friends with the boys; it's just that we weren't the sort of friends who would hang out during Free Time. EXCEPT NOW SOME OF US WERE. And it became Makayla, Brianna, and Abby's official duty to report back exactly what was happening in Bunk 8.

Of course, most of the things they reported were things we already knew. (Like that Jason and Vikas had armpit hair. That was pretty obvious from Swim.) But some things were new—like that Jason had a mustache that he shaved every Thursday or that Alex and Lucas spent twenty minutes a day hanging from the chin-up bar, hoping it would make them taller. And then of course there were the things we learned that we wish we hadn't. Like that Sam, Owen, and Brian had a contest going to see which of them could avoid showering the longest before one of the counselors threw them in. Luckily, by the next summer all three of them had developed an affinity for soap and water, but WE WERE ALL HAPPY NOT TO BE LIVING IN BUNK 8 THAT YEAR!

welcome to the CIT BOYS' BOOK TAKEOVER!

And in case you're wondering, the CIT boys are living in **the CIT bunk**. That's right: Unlike the girls, who are living in the Twelves' bunk, we're far, far away from Bunk 8, where we spent that fateful summer. We're sleeping on REAL BEDS. With real mattresses and everything. The life of luxury. What does that have to

do with The Book? Nothing. We just want to rub it in.

> By "far, far away," we mean two bunks away, obviously.
> —Vikas

What are we doing with The Book?
TAKING OVER! Why? Just like the girls of Bunk 9 were curious about what was going on in the bunk next door, you probably are too. But no way are we letting Brianna and Jenna write our history. If you want to know whether it was Sam, Owen, or Brian who won the no-shower contest, you've got to get it from the source.

> This might not be an <u>official</u> Book hostage situation, but if you mention one more time that you're living in the CIT bunk and we're not, we're sending in a SWAT team to recover it. —EMMA L.

> OK, OK, we also stole The Book because we want to make sure we have the facts right on what's happening in Bunk 9. —Alex

To start, let's go back in time to when we were living in Bunk 8. (You know, when we were twelve. Not when we were CITs.)

Other than Jason and Vikas, who were already well on their way to becoming men, the rest of us pretty much looked like this:

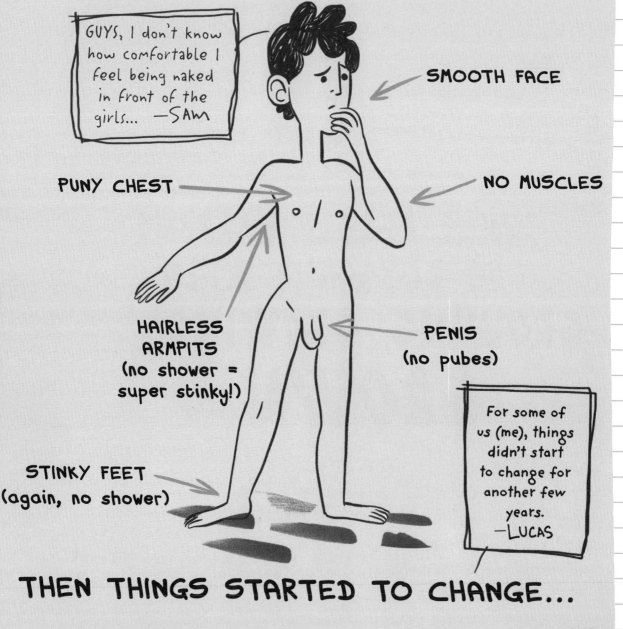

GUYS, I don't know how comfortable I feel being naked in front of the girls... —SAM

SMOOTH FACE

PUNY CHEST

NO MUSCLES

HAIRLESS ARMPITS (no shower = super stinky!)

PENIS (no pubes)

For some of us (me), things didn't start to change for another few years. —LUCAS

STINKY FEET (again, no shower)

THEN THINGS STARTED TO CHANGE...

Many of the changes that girls go through during puberty are the **same** for boys. Just like girls, boys will experience an increase in hormones, they'll sprout hair in new places, their reproductive system will develop, they'll grow taller and have some pimples pop up, and they'll have new feelings and emotions. But if all that is the same, how come men and women look so different? Here's what **REALLY** happens to boys—and when.

> One thing that's different? Boys' voices change and get deeper.
> —Jason

> Sometimes boys will even see a little growth in their chest area that resembles breasts, but that usually disappears by the time puberty is over. —OWEN

~~WHAT REALLY HAPPENS TO BOYS—AND WHEN~~
GROWING, GROWING, GROWN

> SUUUUUPER creative headline, guys. Can we try a little harder for the sake of The Book? —GRACE

First things first: Most boys start going through puberty between the ages of nine and fourteen. On average, that's a year after girls start going through puberty. That's right, **you ladies have a full year's head start.** If it seems like you're towering over the boys when you first start going through puberty, it's because you probably are. Eventually we catch up, but for a while things look a little uneven.

at twelve!

at sixteen!

So HOW did we get from point A to point B?
We turn to Sam for an illustrated demonstration:

Nope. No way, no how. I've already appeared naked here once. It's 100 percent not happening again. —SAM

I VOLUNTEER AS TRIBUTE!! —Brian

OK, FINE, we turn to Brian for an illustrated demonstration:

137

Before puberty, boys look like, well, boys.

You girls won't notice this change because it happens underneath our clothes. —Nate

But at some point, our testicles begin to get a bit bigger. They hang lower, too, and a few pubic hairs grow around the base of our penis. It's the male reproductive system gearing up so it too can make babies.

Soon after, we start to grow. We can grow four inches a year during puberty, but the first things to grow are our hands and feet.

DON'T WORRY— WE WON'T ALL LOOK LIKE BRIAN!

I'm offended that you don't all **WANT** to look like me! —Brian

Just like you get more pubic hair, we do too.

Our penis grows larger and our voice gets deeper. While our voice is changing, it sometimes **CRACKS**. Oops! Sorry about that.

As puberty continues, we get underarm hair and some facial hair. We also start growing chest hair, the hair on our arms and legs gets thicker, and we gain more muscle. We're practically adults!

Every boy will go through the same stages of puberty, but just like you're all different, **we're all different too.** What does that mean? Some of us will be tall and some of us will be short. Some of us will be very hairy, and some of us will hardly be hairy at all. We might have broad shoulders or a thick middle, skinny arms or a lot of muscle, clear skin, acne, or something in between, and underneath our clothes we all look different too! **There are 3.5 billion varieties of us, just like there are 3.5 billion varieties of you.**

COPY THAT

(OR, THE REPRODUCTIVE SYSTEM)

You already know how the female reproductive system works, but what about the male reproductive system? Unlike the female reproductive system, which is mostly on the inside, the male reproductive system is all **out in the open**. Well, under our underwear. Its main parts? The penis, scrotum, testicles, and urethra.

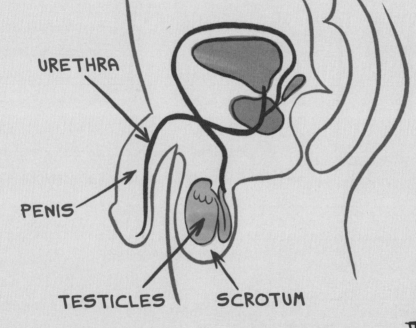

URETHRA

PENIS

TESTICLES

SCROTUM

Until puberty, these parts are just hanging out (except the urethra, which is the tube that urine travels through on its way out of the body). However, when males start going through puberty, their hormones increase and the body gets ready to be able <u>to make a baby.</u>

Whoa, whoa, let's not get ahead of ourselves!! —Alex

That increase in hormones causes the body to start producing sperm—tiny tadpole-looking cells that are made in the testicles (or testes)—that later mixes with fluids inside the body to create something called semen. It exits the body through the urethra—the same tube that carries urine—and out of the penis. This is called ejaculation. As for the scrotum's role? It's the testicles' house, and, like any good house, it has **climate control** to keep the sperm cool so they function properly. That's why it's outside the body.

> Definitely lacking in climate control? The CIT bunk. —LUCAS

When a male's sperm meets a woman's egg, it sometimes fertilizes it, which makes a baby.

> Terrifying! —Brian

A PRONUNCIATION GUIDE TO IMPORTANT PARTS
by Vikas (that's vi-KAAS)

Penis: PEE-nis

Testicle: TEST-ti-cul

Testes: TES-tees

Scrotum: SCRO-tum

Semen: SEE-men

Urethra: you-REETH-ruh

Ejaculation: Ee-jack-you-LAY-shun

THE CIT BOYS' LIST OF

Penises come in two varieties—CIRCUMCISED and UNCIRCUMCISED. At birth, a penis is uncircumcised, which means it has a piece of skin, called a <u>FORESKIN</u>, covering it. Some parents, often for religious, medical, or cultural reasons, choose to circumcise their child, meaning they have the foreskin removed. A circumcised penis looks a little like a mushroom head. An uncircumcised penis looks a little like a mushroom head wearing a turtleneck. Neither one is better or worse than the other—just different. —OWEN

Usually the penis is <u>FLACCID</u> (that's FLA-sid), meaning it is soft and hangs pointing down, close to the body. However, sometimes blood flows into the penis and it becomes erect. During an <u>ERECTION</u> (that's er-EK-shun), the penis enlarges and stiffens. —Nate

Boys can get erections even as babies, but thanks to hormones, during puberty they occur much more frequently and often aren't in our control. They can happen during Afternoon Swim, on a nature hike, during Camp-Wide Movie Night, or in the middle of Kitchen Patrol. —Alex

Luckily, by the time we finish going through puberty, those spontaneous erections are mostly a thing of the past. After that we have much better control over if and when they happen. —Vikas

The penis and testicles are EXTREMELY sensitive. Please be very, VERY careful during dodgeball. Also during kickball, soccer, Capture the Flag, Red Rover, and Marco Polo. Better yet, just <u>be careful</u> ALL the time. —Jason

PENIS PUBERTY FACTS

Until we get it all under control, though, those erections can be <u>embarrassing</u>. I've used a towel, a backpack, a book, a sweatshirt, my knees, a table, a fence, and Jason to hide an unwanted erection. —SAM

Wait, WHAT?
—Jason

Yeah, it was during the Camp-Wide Sing-Along the summer we were fourteen. Everyone was standing in a giant circle with three rows, and I was in the front. I just kind of moved behind you so you'd block me... —SAM

Penises come in a <u>variety of shapes and sizes</u>. They can be long or short, skinny or wide; they can be straight or curved; they can have big balls (that's another word for testicles) or little balls, and any combination of these things. —Brian

Boys (and men) also come in a variety of shapes and sizes. Being broad- or narrow-shouldered, tall or short, or hairy- or smooth-faced doesn't make you any less or more of a man. —Alex

Your height has nothing to do with how big or small your penis is. Neither does anything else—like your shoulders, chest, facial hair, voice, or shoe size. —LUCAS

Sometimes it's hard not to worry about your penis and how it compares to other penises. —SAM

Not just your penis! We worry about how everything measures up. Whether we go through puberty early or late, whether we end up big or small, we're just as insecure about these things as you are. —Nate

I LOVE MY PENIS!!!! —Brian

OMG, GUYS!!!! You can't spend <u>TWO PAGES</u> talking about penises. NO ONE wants to hear it. You have to include other aspects of puberty. You know, like EMOTIONS. —Brianna

FINE. EMOTIONS.

With those hormones suddenly rushing through our bodies, puberty means that (just like you girls) **we guys are experiencing a million new things.** Not only is our physical appearance changing, but we're also starting to notice girls (or boys) in new ways. When you combine those new feelings with the unpredictability of our bodies, it's a RECIPE FOR DISASTER.

> I didn't really notice the girls in a new way. And then I was worried something was wrong with me. But everyone is different, and there's no right or wrong way to feel. —SAM

In fact, want to know a secret? The boys in Bunk 8 are **terrified** of YOU. Scared stiff. Petrified. How do we know? We've been there. Don't believe us? Here is a list of everything we were scared of that summer (and are still a little scared of now):

1. **YOU!** Really. Girls' head start on puberty means most of you already look kind of like women, while we still look a lot like boys. Pretty intimidating.

2. **YOU!** Honestly. We're scared you'll reject us. We're scared you'll laugh at us (instead of with us). We're scared we'll say/do the wrong thing. We're scared we'll say/do the right thing but won't know what to say/do next.

3. **YOU!** Sincerely. We're worried you won't think we're cute, or that you'll notice our acne or that we smell bad, or that you'll think we're too skinny or too fat or too short or too tall or too shy or too loud or not smart

enough or too smart. And we're worried that when we do finally work up the courage to be near you, our voice will crack. Or even worse: We'll get a surprise erection.

> It's no secret that I had a crush on Makayla from the beginning of camp. But it took me two weeks to work up the courage to talk to her, another two weeks to ask her if she'd be my girlfriend, and another two weeks after that to figure out how to get her to hold hands with me. And by that point camp was almost over. —Nate

Our emotions aren't ALL about you, though. **We're also worried about one another**. Are we going through puberty fast enough? Will we ever get as hairy as Jason, or be as fast as Nate, and what if those things don't happen? Another thing that happens as a result of increased hormones is that we get big mood swings, can act a little aggressive, and sometimes behave recklessly and impulsively. Why? Our brain hasn't adjusted to its new normal yet, making our actions and emotions difficult to control. If that sounds familiar, it's because your hormones are having a similar effect on you. The good news is that once we finish going through puberty, our bodies and our brains calm down.

> One of the biggest challenges is learning to control our impulses. Otherwise we come THISCLOSE to getting kicked out of camp for stealing all of the mattresses in the bunk except our own and putting them in the lake. —Jason and Brian

We need to return The Book to its rightful owners, but first, who won the no-shower contest? We're sorry to say it was a three-way tie. Our counselors planned a sneak water attack on Owen, Brian, and Sam at the exact same time. They got an outdoor scrubbing before being thrown into the showers with all their clothes on.

Camp Silver Moon
WEEK 6

IN WHICH EMMA R. AND JENNA MESMERIZE THE GROUP WITH A LITTLE HELP FROM A WIZARD NAMED HARRY, AND **EVERYONE IS IN NEED OF A GOOD NIGHT'S SLEEP.**

We know what you're thinking: Seven weeks at Camp Silver Moon without your parents means seven weeks of staying up all night playing Truth or Dare and eating only dessert. How do we know? **Because we were thinking it too**. That summer we BARELY SLEPT, and by the middle of August, the lack of sleep was taking its toll. We weren't homesick, we weren't scared of the dark, and it wasn't the raccoons that scurried around in the attic above our bunk (although they didn't help matters). No, it was because Jenna and Emma R. read to us EVERY NIGHT from Lights Out until midnight.

Even though we had all already read them, we were working our way through the entire Harry Potter series. All 4,224 pages in seven weeks, 86 pages a night. Each night we would form a circle in the middle of the bunk with our flashlights. Some of us sat on the floor, some of us would sprawl out on bottom bunks. Emma R. and Jenna would trade off chapters until we hit 86 pages. They were spectacular readers. Emma R. read in a calm, steady voice that reminded us of home. Jenna, who is a natural actress, read each page as if she were at a movie audition. Add to that a weekly care package from Abby's grandmother stuffed with home-baked cookies, miniature candy bars, and caramel popcorn, and it was the perfect way to end each day.

Of course it made starting the next one infinitely harder. We were heading to breakfast with OUR EYES BARELY OPEN, and before week 6 of camp was

over, Grace, Sage, and Emma R. were in the infirmary.

As we quickly learned, staying awake all night and filling up on Abby's grandmother's snickerdoodles left almost half of us in the infirmary and the others headed in that direction. It was time to **take matters into our own hands**. After all, we couldn't be successful members of the Sisterhood without putting our BEST SELVES FORWARD. And taking matters into our own hands meant **EATING RIGHT, EXERCISING, AND RESTING UP.**

Without one of our readers, we all caught up on sleep. It helped that Julia and Collette put us on a strict schedule. For the next week, they sat in the middle of the room each night until every last one of us had fallen asleep. There was no talking after Lights Out, no whispering, no blinking.

When Grace, Sage, and Emma R. came back from the infirmary, we moved our reading to our afternoon rest hour. We didn't make up for lost time, and by the last day of summer, we still had half of book seven to go, but the next summer we picked up right where we'd left off. More important, WE WERE HEALTHY.

WHICH WAS GOOD, BECAUSE OUR SUMMER MAY HAVE BEEN WINDING DOWN, BUT IT WAS FAR FROM OVER.

My dads sent a weekly care package too! Only theirs were full of raisins and rice cakes. No one was excited to get THAT. —Jenna

WHAT'S FOR DINNER?

Whether you've been fixing your own meals for years or you can't even find the kitchen at your house, the older you get, the more you'll have to take responsibility for your own nutrition. You probably already know that food makes your body go. It's like the battery for your flashlight, the electricity for the stereo in the counselor area, the wood for the campfire, the gasoline for... There's no gasoline at Camp Silver Moon, but you get the idea. You need food in order to function properly. But just like you wouldn't put AAA batteries in a mega flashlight or keep a campfire going with kindling, **the type of food you eat is as important as eating itself.** So how do you make the best choices when it comes to food?

> I want it on the record that I had NOTHING to do with these terrible analogies. —EMMA L.

Balance Things Out

> NOT a real food group. —GRACE

While it's tempting to eat only things in the *Cookie Food Group,* **BALANCE IS KEY** when it comes to staying healthy. A mix of proteins, vegetables, fruits, grains, and dairy will help you stay awake through Morning Meeting, rock the Ropes Course, and avoid the infirmary. Even if you don't manage to get all of the food groups in every meal, you should have some of each throughout the day.

WHAT IT DOES

Protein

Protein gives you the ▮▮▮▮▮ to go, go, go! Think of it as your secret weapon in a boys-against-girls game of Capture the Flag.

Vegetables

Your best bet for vitamins and minerals, veggies will help keep you full of ▮▮▮▮▮▮▮ and far from the infirmary.

Fruits

Like vegetables, fruits are full of ▮▮▮▮▮▮▮ Plus they contain natural sugars that can give you a burst of energy without the crash that comes with the processed sugar found in foods like snickerdoodles.

Grains

Grains—specifically whole grains—are good for your heart. They're also full of ▮▮▮▮ to help your digestive system stay on track. Eat them to keep your bunkmates from yelling at you for hogging the toilet.

Dairy

Dairy is full of ▮▮▮▮▮▮ for strong bones and protein for energy. In other words, the milk cooler should be your first stop in the dining hall each morning.

A FEW CHOICES		ANYTHING ELSE?
Salmon	Beans	When it comes to protein, lean is best. Choose chicken over beef, white meat over dark, and baked over fried. And while dairy gets its own group, it's a great source of protein, especially for vegetarians.
Tuna	Dairy	
Chicken	Peanut butter	
Eggs	Nuts	
Tofu	Turkey	

Spinach	Broccoli	For the best nutrition, go for color when it comes to vegetables—leafy greens, bright reds, and lots of orange. And while technically tomatoes, bell peppers, and avocados are fruits, we're listing them here anyway.
Kale	Avocados	
Carrots	Sweet potatoes	
Tomatoes	Bell peppers	

Apples	Bananas	Fruit is portable and easy to eat, making it a great snack choice if you need a pick-me-up between meals. In other words, don't hesitate to stop at the mulberry tree on your way back to Bunk 9 after Swim. Just avoid dried fruit when possible, as its sugar content is much higher than in fresh fruit.
Oranges	Grapefruit	
Blueberries	Mulberries	

Whole-wheat bread	While it's tempting to load up on pancakes, pasta, and sugary cereal, refined grains such as white rice, white flour, and white bread lack the fiber and nutrients that their whole-grain counterparts have.
Oatmeal	
Whole-grain cereal	
Brown rice	
Quinoa	
Air-popped popcorn	

Yogurt	Choose low-fat milk products whenever possible, as cream-based dairy products (that's ice cream, cream cheese, and butter) are short on calcium. And if dairy doesn't agree with your stomach, look for soy or nut alternatives with added calcium or lactose-free and fortified rice milk.
Milk	
Cheese	

151

making the most of the
CAMP SILVER MOON DINING HALL

It's easy to make good choices when Leanne, the camp chef, makes a delicious tofu and vegetable stir-fry with brown rice. But what do you do on days when the dreaded tuna casserole is on the menu?

BREAKFAST

✸ Yogurt with granola and a sliced banana

✸ Hard-boiled egg with spinach, avocado, and cheddar cheese, and a side of cantaloupe

✸ Oatmeal with milk and blueberries

LUNCH

✸ Tuna salad made with avocado instead of mayonnaise, baby spinach, and tomato on whole-grain bread

✸ PB&B (that's a peanut butter and banana sandwich) on whole-wheat bread, plus raw broccoli, carrots, and cherry tomatoes with tahini dressing

✸ Turkey sandwich with cheddar, lettuce, tomato, and mustard on whole-grain bread

(Hint: Save your taste buds and find something else!) Here are some easy ideas for a healthy breakfast, lunch, dinner, and in-between, when you need to take charge of your own meals. Just always ask an adult before using the oven or stove.

Most nights at my house we were eating takeout. Delicious, and SERIOUSLY lacking in nutrition. When I turned thirteen, I did a family kitchen takeover. Now I make dinner for the family every weeknight, except Thursdays, when I have hip-hop. That's still pizza night. —Abby

DINNER

☆ Vegetarian southwest salad bowl with black beans, corn, tomatoes, bell peppers, shredded cheese, and a light chipotle-mayo dressing over brown rice

☆ Quinoa bowl with tomato, feta cheese, whole-wheat pita chips, and walnuts

☆ Salad-bar raid: baby spinach, tomatoes, bell peppers, mushrooms, cucumbers, chickpeas, cheese, and a little olive oil and lemon

IN-BETWEENS

☆ Apple slices topped with peanut butter

☆ Orange slices and a handful or two of almonds

☆ Baby carrots and bell peppers dipped in hummus

SIZING THINGS UP

Eating a balanced diet is the first step to staying healthy. The next step is knowing *how much to eat*. While everyone needs different amounts of food depending on their age, height, and amount of physical activity, here are a few guidelines to get you started:

☆ **USE YOUR HANDS!** One portion of grains, fruits, or vegetables should be about the size of your fist, while a portion of protein or dairy should be the size of your palm.

☆ **DIVIDE AND CONQUER!** Split your plate into four parts. (And yes, they should be even!) Two sections should be for vegetables and fruit, one should be for protein or dairy, and one should be for grains.

☆ **LISTEN TO YOUR BODY!** Eat when you're hungry, stop when you're full, and don't skip meals. And remember to pace yourself. Unless you're late to Music Under the Big Tree, there's no need to scarf down your lunch. It takes 20 minutes for your brain to tell your stomach it's stuffed.

It's hard not to overeat when you're starving. If you keep running to the dining hall and piling your plate sky-high, you may need to eat more frequently. Try munching on an apple, some nuts, or cut-up veggies between meals. Eating five smaller meals a day instead of three big ones may be better for your body. —Makayla

WHAT FOOD GROUPS ARE DESSERT & FRENCH FRIES IN?

Unfortunately, dessert and potato chips don't belong to ANY food group. But that doesn't mean you have to give them up forever. After all, food should be **A PLEASURE, NOT A PUNISHMENT.** If you eat a healthy diet most of the time, there's no reason you can't treat yourself occasionally. Whether it's pizza or doughnuts, **everything is OK in moderation.**

> I would eat pizza, fries, and fried chicken for breakfast, lunch, and dinner if I could—the greasier the better. Rather than debating at every meal whether or not it's OK to eat something, I designate one day a week for unhealthy eating, and only if I've gotten all my veggies in the rest of the week. It helps me stay on track, and gives me a reward for all that spinach and kale. —GRACE

SWEET TALKING

You don't need us to tell you that *sugar is delicious.* Brownies, soda, Abby's grandmother's snickerdoodles... no one wants to live in a world without **SNICKERDOODLES!** So why exactly are we supposed to avoid something so great?

When you eat sugar, a few things happen. First, it sends a message to your brain that says, "Gimme, gimme, gimme more." Then your body converts the **SUGAR TO ENERGY**, but because sweetened foods have more sugar than your body can use, it stores **what's left as FAT**. And that "gimme more" factor means more and more fat. All of that extra fat leads to health problems down the road. As for that energy? It sounds good, but IT'S FAKE. That initial burst you feel quickly *leaves you crashing*.

That doesn't mean you can't eat sugar at all—natural sugars found in fruit and milk are perfectly good. It's the *added* sugars you want to avoid. So if you're craving something sweet, try strawberries, watermelon, or unsweetened applesauce instead of brownies, soda, or snickerdoodles. And don't forget—almost everything is OK in moderation. So long as you don't make it a habit, it's OK to enjoy a snickerdoodle every once in a while.

VS

FEELING HANGRY

Yes, you read that correctly. If you get extra-irritable and cranky when you need to eat, you might suffer from **HANGER, OR "HUNGER ANGER."** And even if you don't get hangry yourself, you've probably been on the receiving end of someone else's hanger, especially if you share a bunk with Jenna. If you notice that everyone in Bunk 9 starts to irk you right before meals, it means you need to **KEEP YOUR BLOOD SUGAR MORE STEADY.** Make a habit of keeping high-protein snacks, like nuts, handy, and munch on them before you snap.

Guilty as charged. Grace has been subjected to my hanger more times than I would like to admit. Now I carry a sandwich bag filled with peanuts in my pocket, and when I start to feel annoyed, I quickly eat a handful (or Grace forces me to). —Jenna

LABELING THINGS

When it comes to making good food choices, knowing what you're putting inside your body is one of the most important things you can do. You can't go wrong with fresh vegetables and fruit, but what about packaged foods? Use these tips to help you eat only the best:

★ **READ THE LABEL.** All packaged foods have a label with both the nutrient content and the ingredient list.

★ **STICK TO INGREDIENTS YOU RECOGNIZE.*** When it comes to the ingredient list, shorter is better, and pronounceable is best. If you see an ingredient list with twenty unrecognizable items on it, chances are it's not going to be great for you.

★ **ORDER MATTERS.** Ingredients are listed from the greatest to the least amount. If you see sugar as one of the first few ingredients, skip that snack and move on.

*The exception to this rule? Sugar, which is both pronounceable and recognizable but should still be avoided whenever possible. —Lea

Sugar isn't always sugar. Look for corn syrup, high-fructose corn syrup, glucose, dextrose, sucrose, fruit juice concentrate, malt syrup, and anything that includes the words SUGAR, SYRUP, or CANE. They're all fancy words for "added sugar." —EMMA L.

Drink Up!

The food you put into your body isn't the only thing that affects your health. Sodas, sports drinks, and bottled teas all contain tons of sugar and sugar substitutes, even the diet or light kinds. Most fruit juices, unless they're fresh, aren't much better. Stick to milk, which has great nutritional value, and drink lots and LOTS of water, which will keep you hydrated and help keep your entire body feeling good.

what about DIETS?

You've probably heard people talk about different kinds of diets: no carbohydrates, protein only, raw foods. Bunk 9 is making its ruling: **WE'RE OFFICIALLY ANTI-DIET.** We think the best way to achieve a healthy lifestyle is through *balance*. That means being aware of what you're putting in your body, eating good things from all of the food groups, and treating yourself to the occasional cookie or side of fries. If you're consistent in eating well, you should never have to cut out entire categories of foods. And don't worry about checking your height and weight at home. Your doctor will weigh and measure you at your yearly checkups and let you know if anything needs to change.

> It can sometimes be hard not to worry about food, your weight, or how you look, even if deep down you know that the best you is YOU! If you find that you are worrying about these things more than you were before, talk to your parents, doctor, or another adult you trust. They can help get you back on the right track! —GRACE

Sage's Guide to Going VEGETARIAN

If you've read <u>Charlotte's Web</u>, you've probably at least thought about becoming a VEGETARIAN—that is, not eating meat. Some people choose to become vegetarian because they care about ANIMAL RIGHTS, others because of the impact eating meat has on the environment. But unless you're born into a vegetarian family, making the transition to vegetarianism can be hard. Especially if beef chili is on the dinner menu three nights a week, like at my house. So how do you make the leap?

Talk to your parents. Chances are, food decisions at home are up to your parents. If you're committed to becoming a vegetarian, you'll **need your parents to be on board.** Come to them with your reasons, as well as a plan for how to make it happen—including meal alternatives and grocery lists.

Be prepared to take over your own food prep. My mom was fine with me becoming a vegetarian. She was less fine with cooking two separate meals or giving up meat herself. That meant **I NEEDED TO START FENDING FOR MYSELF.** I learned how to make a few basic dishes, which I ate on nights when she cooked meat, and we compromised on some things, such as switching to vegetarian chili.

Be OK with going it alone. Just like you have the right to choose vegetarianism, your family has the right to choose to keep eating meat. You can talk to them about your reasons, but accept that ultimately the choice is theirs.

Watch your nutrition. Giving up meat means cutting out a significant source of protein as well as nutrients such as vitamin B12 and iron. Make sure you're still taking care of yourself by paying *extra attention* to nutrients and adding them in through other means.

Go slow. If you want to give up eating meat but are worried it will be difficult, think about doing a test run. Suggest to your parents that you give vegetarianism a one-month try before fully committing. Or try it at Camp Silver Moon before doing it year-round. You can also try **PROGRESSIVELY CUTTING OUT** different kinds of meat, starting with red meat, then chicken, then fish.

WORK iT!

Morning Swim, the Ropes Course, Capture the Flag, volleyball, nature hikes. If it seems like Bunk 9 is constantly on the go, that's because we are. Staying healthy is about more than eating right; it's also about getting regular exercise. But why do you need to move and what are some of the best ways to do it (especially if your favorite activity is Music Under the Big Tree)?

How much exercise does "daily exercise" consist of? At least thirty minutes of moderate movement a day. But it doesn't have to be all at once. You can run from the bunk to the dining hall in the morning, swim to the dock and back in the afternoon, and go for a stroll through camp in the evening. —Lea

1. It keeps you IN SHAPE. You've all heard that practice makes perfect. The same goes for exercise—the more you do it, the easier it will become. Keeping your body strong means it will be that much easier to win the canoe race across Lake Silver Moon, get through the Ropes Course Challenge, or chase the boys when they steal The Book.

2. It keeps you HEALTHY. It might not seem like a big deal now, but exercising today can help you be healthy tomorrow. The chances of developing conditions such as heart disease and osteoporosis later in life can be decreased by staying active. Working out also helps lower your blood sugar.

3. It keeps you HAPPY. Have you ever felt a rush of excitement after a game of basketball or a night of dancing? Or have you noticed that going for a walk or a bike ride when you're grumpy or sad can make your mood better? That's because exercise causes your body to release chemicals called ENDORPHINS, which make you feel good. In other words, working out can make you happy. And that will make all of Bunk 9 happy!

When it's been raining for three days and everyone in Bunk 9 is getting on each other's nerves, Emma R. and Abby lead us in a bunk-wide dance party. I have two left feet, but even I end up feeling better afterward.

—Brianna

But I Really, REALLY Hate Sports...

Sage might be the star of her track team and Grace can kick anyone's butt in volleyball (as long as she hasn't stuffed her bra), but **we get it**: Not everyone loves to exercise. So what do you do if you'd rather be doing just about anything else?

1. **Find things you do like to do.** If team sports aren't for you, try *solo sports* such as running, swimming, or biking. If team AND solo sports aren't for you, try other activities that involve moving, such as dance, yoga, Pilates, or hiking. —Abby

2. **Look for hidden exercise in everyday activities.** You don't have to join a sports team or take an exercise class to get moving. **Going for a walk, taking the stairs, or giving a friend a piggyback ride** to Arts & Crafts all count as exercise. —Makayla

3. **Go slow.** If you're used to spending all of Free Time sitting under the Big Tree, taking up thirty minutes of jogging a day might burn you out fast. Start with ten to fifteen minutes of exercise a few days a week, and SLOWLY WORK YOUR WAY UP TO MORE. —Lea

4. **Find a friend.** It's always easier to stay motivated when you **have a buddy.** Emma R. and I go for a walk around camp every day during Free Time. It gives us a chance to talk about the day and gets us moving at the same time. —EMMA L.

> My top five Camp Silver Moon activities: Arts & Crafts, Rest Hour, Music Under the Big Tree, Drama, dinner. My bottom five camp activities: EVERYTHING else. —Jenna

> How I finally started exercising? BABYSITTING. Chasing after a five-year-old for two hours every afternoon got me moving and was a great way to earn $$$. —Jenna

YOU ARE GETTING SLEEPY. VERY, VERY SLEEPY.

Don't worry, we're not about to hypnotize you into thinking you're a chicken. We already tried that with Grace, and it didn't work. We just want to talk about the importance of sleep. After all, we want the members of the Sisterhood to be awake!

> Nope, it didn't work for even a second! But I did pretend for five minutes and it TOTALLY freaked them out. —GRACE

WHY SLEEP?

Just like food acts as a battery that helps you go, sleep recharges you at night. While you sleep, your body rests in preparation for the next day. It's like *having a clean slate every morning.* Not only that, but your brain does a lot of its problem solving while you sleep. So if you get a full night's rest, you might just wake up having figured out the best way across the Ropes Course Challenge.

> That's it! I'm sleeping from the moment we hit Lights Out until five minutes before breakfast every day until I manage to cross the Ropes Course. —Lea

How Much Harry Potter Can We Get Away With and STILL FUNCTION?

NOT MUCH. While you need less sleep than you did when you were a baby, you still need about ten or eleven hours of rest to recharge and help you grow. So if Lights Out is at 9 p.m., you should plan on being in your own bed and deep inside your sleeping bag by 9:30.

AND IF WE DON'T SLEEP? Not only will you be tired if you don't sleep, but your body and brain will start to *break down*. Missing sleep can make you cranky and forgetful, and it can make it impossible to do everyday things.

BRIANNA'S GUIDE TO NOT SLEEPING

Insomnia, or the inability to sleep, makes it hard to fall asleep and/or stay asleep. If, like me, you're tossing and turning all night, try these tips:

1. Breathe deeply. Establish a rhythm with your breathing to help calm your body.

2. Clear your mind. Try to let go of anything that might have bothered you during the day. It might even help to visualize yourself sleeping!

3. Wear earplugs. It might feel weird the first few times, but blocking out Makayla's snoring might just do the trick.

Nope, not me, not guilty!
—Makayla

4. Eat a banana, or drink a warm glass of milk. Bananas and milk both have a chemical in them that helps promote sleep.

5. Avoid naps. It might be tempting to sleep through Rest Hour, but resist the urge. A midday nap will put your body on a cycle that's hard to break.

6. Stay away from screens during the hour before bed, including your phone, TV, tablet, and computer. Easy enough at camp, where we're electronics free, but during the year try reading a hardcover or paperback book after you tuck yourself in.

THE BEST YOU IS... YOU!

You've probably noticed that even though Bunk 9 eats well and exercises (yes, even Jenna), every one of us looks different. That's because everyone's body is DIFFERENT. Sage will always be short and Makayla will always be tall. Brianna is naturally curvy, and Abby is naturally thin. Emma L. will probably always gain weight in her hips, and Emma R. will probably always gain weight in her stomach. Lea's broad-shouldered, and Jenna is not, and Grace is somewhere in-between. In other words, **WE'RE ALL UNIQUE**.

As you grow up, your body will likely change in unexpected ways. Eating right and exercising may change some things—they can add muscle or take off a few pounds—but they won't change the natural shape of your body. And that's a good thing! After all, variety makes things INTERESTING. What does that mean for you? Eat healthy foods, stay active, and get plenty of rest so you can be the absolute best version of YOU!

Camp Silver Moon
WEEK 7

IN WHICH EVERYONE PUTS ON THEIR BEST OUTFITS, AND **ABBY ADDS ANOTHER "FIRST"** TO OUR SUMMER.

On the second-to-last night of camp, **ABBY HAD HER FIRST KISS.** And even though Makayla and Nate had been going out for a few weeks, Abby's first kiss was also Bunk 9's very first kiss. Every single one of us, including our counselors, Julia and Collette, and the

SITE OF ABBY'S FIRST KISS

entire boys' bunk, was there to *witness it.* It helped that it happened on the path between Bunk 8 and Bunk 9.

See, a few days earlier, Lucas had asked Nate to ask Makayla to ask Abby if she would go with him to the **Twelves-Thirteens Dance.** And while Abby and Brianna had already promised each other they'd go together, Brianna was willing to sacrifice having a date for Abby's sake. (Not that Brianna let anyone forget her big sacrifice.) Of course, none of the rest of us except Makayla had dates either.

On the night of the big dance, **WE ALL GOT DRESSED UP.** Jenna and Grace went as twins and both wore green dresses. Brianna brushed her hair and Abby didn't. Collette let us borrow her makeup and also showed us how to apply it. Even Sage put on a necklace. And then at 7:15 we walked down to the rec hall with the boys. (We're pleased to report the boys had put on clean shirts, and a few of them even had **GEL** in their hair!)

One of the Thirteens' counselors was DJing, and Emma R. taught us all how to do The Robot. **The last song was a SLOW SONG**, and most of our group formed a big circle and swayed. Emma L. wanted to ask Vikas to dance with her but couldn't work up the nerve. But Makayla and Nate danced together. So did Abby and Lucas. (Not a single one of us danced with any of the Thirteens.)

And so no one was surprised when two nights later, at the *Twelves' end-of-summer campfire*, Lucas sat down next to Abby. At the end of the night, even though we were already right outside our bunk, Lucas asked Abby if he could walk her home. Collette and Julia ushered us inside to give them some privacy. But there's no such thing as privacy at Camp Silver Moon. The girls peered out the windows of Bunk 9. The boys hovered on the porch of Bunk 8. And under our watchful eyes...

ABBY AND LUCAS SHARED THEIR FIRST KISS. NATURALLY, WE ALL CHEERED FOR THEM. IT WAS THE PERFECT END TO THE PERFECT SUMMER.

Tread CAREFULLY Through Bunk 9

Jenna and Grace are in a fight, Makayla and Abby are whispering about boys while Brianna feels left out, and the Emmas are crying because camp is almost over. Only Lea and Sage seem happy, and they're not even IN Bunk 9. They're on the porch, writing notes in each others' journals.

Your body isn't the only thing that changes during puberty—your feelings and emotions change too. Some of them don't, of course—you still feel happy, sad, angry, grumpy, scared, and excited, just like you have since you were a baby. But your emotions might feel more **INTENSE**, and they may change more quickly than before. There may be NEW feelings too, such as attraction to other people.

So how do you get through friendships, parents that drive you crazy, and new crushes when your emotions feel as SHAKY as standing up in a canoe in the middle of Lake Silver Moon?

MAKE NEW FRIENDS, BUT KEEP THE OLD

You've probably noticed that friendships change. You might have a fight with your best friend, or perhaps you're simply drifting apart. Maybe your bestie sends you a funny link that reminds you exactly why she's your number one. Or your duo becomes a trio. You might even realize how much you have in common with someone you barely talked to before. But while **all relationships CHANGE over time**, knowing that doesn't make it any easier if you don't want a single thing to be different. So what do you do about the bumps on the road?

169

BESTIES

A good friendship shouldn't require much work—after all, the best friendships are ones that are **mutual and allow you to BE YOURSELF**. But it's still nice to be reminded every once in a while that you're special. Show your best friend how much you care by bringing her a book when she's sick in the infirmary, making her a playlist, or helping her practice for the Ropes Course Challenge.

> I know how much Abby loves to cook, so the summer we were thirteen, I gave her a notebook with Chef Leanne's favorite recipes from the dining hall. That way she could re-create camp year-round.
> —Makayla

COLD SHOULDER

Even the best of friends can drift apart. Sometimes our interests change, and sometimes we simply outgrow friendships. Let's be honest: IT SUCKS. Especially if you're the one being outgrown. But while you can't force someone to stay friends with you, you also don't have to stay miserable if your best friend starts to feel a lot less "best." Look around for someone else you have something in common with. Be brave and ask a new group of girls to hang out during Free Time. You might be surprised by what you find! And even if it takes some time, **eventually you'll connect with someone new.** We promise.

> Abby and I were friends since kindergarten, but by the time we started going to camp, we weren't hanging out as much. Then she immediately clicked with Brianna and Makayla. My first week was MISERABLE. I was homesick and friendless. Then I began sitting with the Emmas at meals and things got better. But it wasn't until this year, when Lea showed up, that I really found a new partner in crime. —SAGE

DRIFTWOOD

BFF. Best. Friends. Forever. Except sometimes you don't want it to be **FOREVER**. If you're outgrowing a friendship, you might feel annoyed, guilty, uncomfortable, or all of the above. But while you don't have to stay in a friendship that's no longer working for you, IT'S IMPORTANT TO BE KIND. Remind yourself of the reasons you became friends in the first place, and let go by gradually spending less time together. You can be direct if your bestie confronts you, but respect the friendship. Remember, being mean is a serious violation of the Rules of the Silver Moon Sisterhood.

> Rules??? Stay tuned! —Lea

Two's COMPANY. Three's a CROWD.

When you're traveling in threes, it's hard not to feel left out sometimes, especially if it seems like the other two have something in common that you don't. Keep your best trio healthy by **resisting the urge to go two against one.** And while it's more than OK for just two of you to hang from time to time, do it without gossiping about your third.

> I definitely felt left out when Makayla had Nate, Abby had Lucas, and I had my sleeping bag. —Brianna

> And I was super worried about getting ditched when Makayla and Brianna talked about periods nonstop and mine was nowhere in sight. —Abby

It's Not Over Till It's OVER

Fights happen, but even the biggest fight doesn't have to be The End. If you're fighting with a friend, take a step back and try to **understand their point of view,** even if you don't agree with it. Give yourself a couple of days to calm down, and ASK YOURSELF if being right is more important than keeping the friendship. And while it may be hard to do, never underestimate the power of reaching out.

I'm sorry

• • •

> Jenna and I didn't speak the entire summer we were thirteen. Not even to say, "Pass the ketchup," and I love ketchup. I'm not sure either of us knows why. Let's just say it was a terrible summer that we both pretend never happened. But a few months after camp, Emma L. was having a slumber party and invited us both. And then one of Jenna's dads gave me a ride home, and I realized how much I missed my best friend. I sent her a text message that night asking if we could meet for berry smoothies. She answered right away, and after a very, very big hug, it was like our fight never happened. —GRACE

GOING SOCIAL

Camp Silver Moon: seven weeks, NO PHONES, NO INTERNET, NO SOCIAL MEDIA. It might seem like torture at first, but it's surprisingly nice. In fact, some of us feel like we want to stay off social media awhile longer. We know, we know, it's fun to see other people's photos and videos—but do we really need to know EXACTLY which slumber parties we weren't invited to? But if a seven-week break was enough, here are a few tips to get you back online on the right foot:

✮ **Be supportive.** Like your friends' posts, but only make positive comments. When it comes to social media, the best rule to practice is the Golden Rule: **Never say or post anything about someone that you wouldn't want posted about yourself.**

✮ **The internet is forever.** And ever. And ever. Think twice (maybe even thrice) before you post. Even if you remove something later, a screenshot may have been captured, so never post, message, or email anything you think you might regret.

✮ **Call "in" instead of "out."** It might be tempting to comment on something you don't like, but take it from us—it will only make things worse. If someone posts something that makes you mad, pick up the phone and call them, old-school, to talk about it.

> I once posted that Makayla was driving me crazy, and even though I took it down less than three minutes later, someone sent it to her. It almost ended our friendship.
> —Brianna

✮ **Stand up for your friends.** If you see someone being hit by mean posts, stick by them. They'll need your support.

✮ **It's never as good as it seems.** Yes, that slumber party looks really fun, and no, you weren't invited, but try to remember that any post captures only one very brief moment in time. Who knows what happened five minutes later.

✮ **Take a break.** Social media should make you feel good about yourself, but it doesn't always work that way. If the posts you see make you feel sad or anxious, take care of yourself and take a break. There's no rule that says you have to be social.

Most social media is harmless, but every once in a while things can get ugly. While it may be hard to do, if you're being bullied online, take your accounts offline, at least temporarily, and tell your parents, teacher, or another adult you're close with—they can provide support and help you figure out what to do next.

What's the most important part of the Silver Moon Sisterhood? **THE SISTERHOOD!** Being a woman is awesome, but it can also be hard work. Which is why it's important to *stick together*. Not only will it make the difficult parts easier, but it will make the good parts a lot more fun. We therefore and hereby present...

RULES OF THE SILVER MOON SISTERHOOD

1. **Kindness first.** You might not be friends with everyone, but you can be kind to everyone. Treat your sisters the way you want them to treat you.

2. **Love yourself.** Whether you have hips that are curvy or straight; boobs that are big or don't exist; a build that is tall, short, or in-between—always celebrate YOU!

3. **Celebrate your sisters.** Just like you're unique, so is everyone else.

4. **Don't gossip.** It's fun to talk to your friends, whether it's squealing over a boy you like or the latest mystery novel. But when it comes to talking about other people, only say the sorts of things you'd want other people to say about you.

5. **Be supportive.** Be a good friend by celebrating first periods, providing comfort during bad breakouts, and lending an ear during good times and bad.

6. You don't have to go to Camp Silver Moon to be part of the Silver Moon Sisterhood; **you just have to embody the spirit.**

PARENTAL CONTROL

The best thing about Camp Silver Moon? Seven weeks of **TOTAL INDEPENDENCE**. OK, maybe not total independence. Your counselors are still going to hit the lights at night and, unfortunately, set an alarm for breakfast. But it's seven weeks of deciding all by yourself what to eat, what to do during Free Time, and whether or not and when to shower. And while there's nothing better than sleeping in your own bed after seven weeks of hearing Makayla snore, the transition back to your parents can be hard. After all, you've been given a taste of freedom, and here's your mom barging through your bedroom door. How do you survive life at home when you just want to be back in Bunk 9?

I don't snore!!! —Makayla

FAMILY TIME

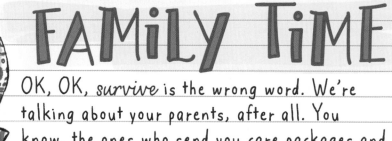

OK, OK, *survive* is the wrong word. We're talking about your parents, after all. You know, the ones who send you care packages and bring your favorite magazines and Chinese food on Visiting Day. But as you get older, your relationship with your family begins to change. Sometimes your mom becomes another friend; other times you can't believe she would wear **THAT HORRIBLE HAT** on Visiting Day. But no matter how embarrassing your parents might be, you can't change the fact that they're family.

175

Just like it helps to show your friends that you care, your family can use a little appreciation too. And while we know spending the weekend with your *dorky younger brother* can be a pain, making time for your family will not only help keep you close as you get older, it will help you communicate when there are bigger things at stake. If your social life is getting in the way, talk to your parents about scheduling time to do things with them. They'll appreciate the fact that you're making an effort and will be more likely to let you go to Emma L.'s Camp Silver Moon Reunion Sleepover.

> My dads and I used to spend every Sunday afternoon together, going on bike rides or playing in the park. But now I want the weekends to see my friends. I asked them if we could switch to a weeknight. They were reluctant at first, but now we cook dinner and play board games every Tuesday night. They like that I'm not complaining, and I like that I still get to spend time with them without giving up my friends. —Jenna

Sister, Sister (or Sister, Brother)

Yes, you have the Silver Moon Sisterhood, but nothing beats the real thing. Siblings are the only people who know exactly how crazy your parents are. Which means no matter how much they make you want to scream, you'll thank us later if you stay on good terms with them. Besides, they make for good backup when you need something from your parents.

> It definitely helps having an older sister to pave the way. Not only does she give great advice about periods and boys, she also fought with my parents about pierced ears, curfews, and screen time, so now I don't have to! —Makayla

INDEPENDENCE DAY

As you get older, you may find that you want more independence. Maybe you want to go to the park without your parents, or get dropped off at school a block away. You might want to keep your bedroom door closed, stop taking harp lessons, or dye your hair green. While your parents ultimately have the final say (we _know_), it definitely helps to talk to them. But take it from us: **There are right—and wrong—ways to talk to your parents.**

RIGHT: Set up a time in advance to talk. Yup, I took harp lessons. It's a _beautiful_ instrument and I STINK at it. When I was thirteen I decided I wanted to quit. I asked my parents if we could have a talk sometime, and we decided on an evening two days later. —Emma R.

WRONG: Spring it on them. When I wanted to dye my hair purple, I wanted to do it that very second. So I asked my mom. First thing in the morning. Before her coffee. Guess who didn't get to dye her hair purple? —Lea

RIGHT: Make a game plan. I wanted to skip my third cousin's wedding for a HIP-HOP DANCE COMPETITION. I made a list of points (I've been practicing nonstop! My cousin won't even notice!) and presented them to my parents. —Abby

WRONG: Scream and shout and let it all out. My parents are the best, but even they drew the line at a coed Camp Silver Moon Reunion Slumber Party. That huge tantrum I threw didn't exactly sway them. —EMMA L.

OFFER TO HELP

More independence? It goes together with more responsibility. That's right: You need to lend a helping hand. Whether it's babysitting The Brat or loading the dishwasher, **showing your parents that you're ready to be more of an adult** will make them more likely to believe it.

> Ugh. I hate babysitting The Brat, but offering to watch my little brother on Sunday mornings was the only way I could convince my parents to let me go to the mall with Jenna on Sunday afternoons. —GRACE

ASK FOR HELP

When it comes down to it, your parents have a lot more experience than you do. Sure, they may not have grown up with the same things you did (hello, smartphones!), but they still know one or two things. And chances are, they want to help you. Even if it's not easy, talk to them about the things that are bothering you. And share the good things too. After all, your parents are your biggest fans.

Feeling Stressed!

One thing that can prevent you from putting the best you forward? STRESS. You know... that feeling you get before the Ropes Course Challenge, when you're worried about making new friends, or when you need to talk to your parents about something BIG. Stress affects you on the inside and out—it can keep you awake at night, cause your skin to break out, wreak havoc on your digestive system, and leave you walking around like a ball of nerves. While avoiding stress completely is impossible, here are a few tips to help you get through it:

☆ **BE PREPARED.** Leaving things to the last minute can put your stomach in knots. Whether you're studying for a test or practicing for the Ropes Course Challenge, try doing a little bit each day for more success, and less stress!

☆ **PRACTICE MAKES PERFECT.** Maybe you need to ask your dad to help you buy a bra. Or you're trying to explain to your BFF why you don't like something she said. If you're gearing up for a conversation you know will be hard, PRACTICE IT IN FRONT OF THE MIRROR or write down what you want to say ahead of time so you have an idea of what's to come.

☆ **SLEEP, BREATHE, AND MEDITATE.** If you're feeling stressed, lack of sleep can make it worse. (Of course, it doesn't help that stress can make you lose sleep!) If you can't catch your ZZZZ'S, find a quiet corner to relax and regroup. Take deep breaths, do some gentle yoga poses, and clear your mind.

☆ **EXERCISE.** Aerobic exercise can help relieve stress and elevate your mood. If you're feeling anxious, *try going for a walk, a jog, or a hike*, or head to your nearest dance class.

179

YOU'RE CRUSHING IT!

Do you get nervous every time Jason sits at your table in the dining hall? Do you keep your fingers crossed you'll be put in the same group as he is for Drama Games? Do you feel your heart pound and your belly tumble when he knocks on the door of Bunk 9 asking to borrow the plunger? If you said yes, yes, and yes, it sounds like you might have a crush. But what exactly is a crush and why does it happen?

> Jason borrows the plunger A LOT. —GRACE

WHAT'S CRUSHING?

When you have a crush on someone, your feelings toward that person are... DIFFERENT. You might get nervous or embarrassed around a crush, or have trouble figuring out what to say. **Your face might turn BRIGHT RED**, your palms and armpits might get suuuuper sweaty, and your pupils may dilate. You might think your crush is the funniest person in the world. And chances are, when you have a crush, you want to be near that person as much as possible. What's going on? It's an uncontrollable rush of hormones that

happens when you're attracted to someone. Usually a crush involves romantic feelings toward another person, but you can also have a friend-crush on someone, especially when you first meet them.

When I first got to Camp Silver Moon, I immediately developed a friend-crush on Sage. I thought her homemade beauty products were the coolest, plus I wished I could be as athletic as she is. Now we're good friends! —Lea

My first crush was on this kid Daniel in my kindergarten class. I crushed on him and he crushed my heart. —Makayla

Can We Choose Our Crushes?

Nope! We're attracted to people for many different reasons, and **having a crush on someone is often entirely out of our control**. Sometimes we like someone because they're funny or kind. Other times we like the way they smell or look. And we hate to admit it, but sometimes we have a crush on someone because everyone else does too. And crushes don't have to make sense. We've had crushes on counselors, celebrities, and even Brian.

I definitely jumped on the bandwagon when it came to having a crush on Nate. After all, if everyone else liked him, it had to be for a reason. —Jenna

I had a big crush on Counselor Matt for most of the summer we were thirteen, even though he was already in college. I felt like he "got" me in a way that most of the people in the group didn't. I was totally heartbroken when his girlfriend showed up on Visiting Day. —SAGE

No way am I admitting to that crush on Brian. —Brianna

ARE CRUSHES ALWAYS ON BOYS?

They don't have to be! While most people are attracted to the opposite sex (for those of you in Bunk 9, the opposite sex = boys), some people find themselves with crushes on people of the same sex. Sometimes that's simply a friend-crush, like Lea had when she first met Sage, and it quickly fades. But other times it's a crush-crush, and the feelings are very real.

You might be confused by a crush on another girl and decide to keep it private until you've had a chance to figure out your feelings, or it may feel totally natural and something you share with your friends right from the start. You might have crushes only on girls, or you might have crushes on girls and boys. If you do find yourself with feelings for other girls, **it's nothing to be worried about**—like we said, you can't choose who you're attracted to. Your crushes, no matter who they're on, should be *celebrated*!

I realized when I was thirteen that all of my crushes were on girls, and exactly zero of my crushes were on boys, which I'm pretty happy about, because no girls I know have ever had a contest to see who could go the longest without showering. —Emma R.

Um, I'm DEFINITELY not celebrating my crush on Brian! —Brianna

What If I Don't Have a Crush on Anyone?

That's OK! Not everyone has crushes. If you don't get tummy-tumbling feelings about other people, **there's nothing wrong with you.** You might get crushes when you're a bit older, and you might not. You can't control who you <u>don't</u> have a crush on any more than you can control who you DO have a crush on!

I LIKE HIM

(OR, WHAT TO DO WHEN YOU HAVE A CRUSH ON SOMEONE)

As we learned from Emma L., getting the same haircut as the boy you like is not the best way to proceed. So what are some of the things you <u>should</u> do if you have a crush on someone?

1. **Tell your crush!** OK, OK, this one is hard, because what if your crush doesn't like you back? But if Lucas hadn't asked Nate to ask Makayla to ask Abby to the dance, then Abby wouldn't have ended the summer with her first kiss. And Lucas wouldn't have either! IF YOU CAN WORK UP THE NERVE (and are pretty sure you'll bounce back if your crush isn't mutual), then find a way to let them know. A few tips to help with the inevitable mortification? Try to **catch your crush privately,** or at the very least without too many people around. Practice what you're going to say before you say it. And don't be too hard on yourself if you chicken out!

2. **Enjoy the feeling.** We know it can sometimes feel like TORTURE to have a crush on someone, especially if you get tongue-tied whenever they're around, but let's be honest: Those stomach *butterflies* are also exciting.

3. Do nothing. There's no rule that states you have to do *anything* about a crush. It's up to you if you tell your crush, or even your BFF.

> I've had crushes I didn't even tell Grace about. —Jenna

> Wait, WHAT!? —GRACE

I Like Him (NOT)

When someone likes you, you might feel happy or flattered. Then again, if you don't have a crush on them, you might not be so thrilled. So how do you let someone down easy when you're just not feeling it? The most important thing is to imagine how you would want to be told if it were the other way around, and to **BE KIND** and respectful. Thank the person for telling you and let them know you're sorry that the feeling isn't mutual. Say it when there aren't too many other people around, and resist the urge to announce it to the whole bunk during Morning Meeting.

He Likes Me!!

What happens when you have a crush on someone and they have a crush on you too? **First, get excited! REALLY, REALLY excited!** Definitely announce THIS at Morning Meeting! What's next? That's up to you. It might mean a date to the dance or a kiss between the bunks. It might mean the two of you are "going out" and really just hang out. It might mean you have a crush on someone who has a crush on you and

nothing else happens. There's no right or wrong way to move forward. Do what feels right to you—and to your crush.

> I was so excited when Nate asked me out, but it really meant we just spent time getting to know each other. We didn't even kiss until two summers later, and by that time we were practically best friends. —Makayla

> Uhhhh, watch who you call your best friend!! —Abby and Brianna

JUST SAY NO (OR YES)

Whether you're getting a hug or a kiss, a pat on the back, or a fist bump, how, where, and if someone touches you is **YOUR CHOICE**. (That goes for your parents, your aunt Edna, Brian and Vikas, Counselor Julia, and Brianna.) If someone touches you in a way you don't like, tell them. If they persist, talk to an adult you trust. And remember, it goes both ways. So if Grace asks you not to hug her, keep your hands off!

HE LIKES ME NOT...

There's nothing worse than liking someone who doesn't like you back. (OK, <u>maybe</u> there are worse things, like the bubonic plague, the apocalypse, or tuna casserole, but it's in the top five for sure. Or at least top ten.) So what's the best way to bounce back?

1. Stay strong. Because it's not literally the apocalypse, you'll survive. We promise.

186

2. **Call up the Sisterhood.** Hello, what is the Sisterhood for if not to help you get over your crush (who was SO not worth it anyway)?

3. **Watch your favorite movie, eat ice cream, and have a pity party of one.** It's OK to be sad, and even to eat ice cream... just don't wallow too long!

4. **Respect your crush's feelings.** We know you may be tempted to convince your crush otherwise, but turning someone down is only slightly less hard than being turned down yourself. Hold your head up high, but don't make your crush's life difficult just because they can't see what they're missing!

> When I finally told Brian I liked him—and he told me he didn't like me back— Counselor Julia set up a girls-only sleeping bag party in the rec hall. We watched <u>Clueless,</u> ate popcorn, and stayed up almost all night. —Brianna

GIVE ME A SMOOCH

Now that we've talked crushes, we know what you're thinking... **YOU WANT THE SCOOP ON ABBY'S FIRST KISS:** how it happened and, more important, how to do it right when it's your turn. Whether your first kiss is at twelve like Abby's, at fourteen like Makayla's, or still to come, like Emma L.'s, dear members of the Silver Moon Sisterhood, we can't tell you ALL of the secrets of womanhood. After all, <u>some things will be infinitely better if you wait patiently and figure them out yourself.</u>

187

As the camp bus pulled out of the parking lot that summer, there wasn't a dry eye among us. Emma R., Jenna, and Brianna were crying on the side of the road while they waited for their parents to pick them up by car. Grace, Emma L., Sage, Abby, and Makayla cried on the bus. We're sure if Lea had been there, she would have been crying too. **We couldn't believe it would be ANOTHER 316 DAYS before all of us were TOGETHER AGAIN.**

We also couldn't believe how worried we'd been about our friendships at the beginning of the summer. True, in many ways we were still different. Brianna was still a head taller than Abby. Makayla still had boobs, and Grace still didn't. **BUT WE HADN'T LET OUR DIFFERENCES TEAR US APART.** We'd celebrated first boyfriends and first periods. We'd comforted each other over stuffed bras and bad zits. **We were there for each other.** We were bosom buddies, breast friends. We were then, and would always be, the **SiLVER MOON SiSTERHOOD.**

ACKNOWLEDGMENTS

First and foremost, thank you to the entire team at Workman for making this book happen, for getting behind it, and for adding your own tips and advice in the margins. I am especially indebted to Justin Krasner, who is an amazing editor and champion, and also had the brilliant idea of setting The Book at Camp Silver Moon, and to Daniel Nayeri for thinking of me for this project in the first place, and for his friendship. Thank you, too, to Meg Hunt for bringing Camp Silver Moon to life, and to Dr. Meryl Newman-Cedar for double-checking my science.

Thank you to all of my friends who were willing to talk to me about their breasts, their periods, and their experiences in puberty, who answered my random texts and emails, and who shared their own stories and advice with me as I was writing. There are too many to name individually, but I am especially grateful to Claudia Goldstein, Rebecca Gorney, and Matthew Longo for reading every word I sent them and giving me their thoughtful feedback, and to Safiya Martinez Connell for her careful notes about hair.

Camp Silver Moon would not exist if it were not for Camp Kinderland; the many summers I spent there helped shape how I grew up and how I learned to think about my body. Thank you to the entire Camp Kinderland family, and to the August 2016 Senior and Fourteen girls, who brainstormed with me, telling me what they wanted to know and what they wish they had known then.

Last, thank you to my family—my parents, Semadar Megged and Natan Nuchi, and my brothers, Haggai and Elisha Nuchi—who have cheered for me every day of my life, and helped me to be my best me.

ADAH NUCHI grew up in New York City and spent her summers at camp, where she learned (almost) everything she needed to know about being a woman. She worked for many years as a children's book editor and now divides her time between writing and going on adventures, which mostly occur on the beach.

MEG HUNT is an illustrator and maker of things. When she's not reading, exploring, or learning, Meg is discovering the world through her illustrations. Previously, she illustrated the book Interstellar Cinderella. Her clients include Scholastic, Chronicle Books, Storey Publishing, Disney, DreamWorks, Coach, and Adobe. She lives and works in Portland, Oregon.